Treatise Concerning the Christian Priesthood

Treatise Concerning the Christian Priesthood

St. Chrysostom

Treatise Concerning the Christian Priesthood

© Lighthouse Church Fathers 2022

Written by: St. Chrysostom
Translated by: Rev. W.R.W. Stephens, M.A. (5 October 1839 – 22 December 1902)
Updated into Modern U.S English: A.M. Overett (b. 1960)

All rights reserved. Without limiting the rights under copyright reserved above, no part of this publication may be reproduced, stored in a retrieval system, or transmitted, in any form or by any means (electronic, mechanical, photocopying, recording or otherwise), without the prior written permission of the copyright owner of this book.

Published by
Lighthouse Publishing
SAN 257-4330
5531 Dufferin Drive
Savage, Minnesota, 55378
United States of America

www.lighyouseebooks.com

INTRODUCTION TO THE TREATISE ON THE PRIESTHOOD.

The events recorded in this celebrated treatise on the Priesthood must have occurred when St. John Chrysostom was about twenty-eight years of age. His father had died when he was a young child; his mother was a devout Christian but had not destined him for the clerical vocation. The great ability which he showed in early youth seemed to mark him out for distinction in one of the learned professions, and at the age of eighteen he began to attend the school of Libanius, the most celebrated sophist of the day, who had won a great reputation as a professor of philosophy and rhetoric, and as an eloquent opponent of Christianity, not only in his native city, Antioch, but also in Athens, Nicomedia, and Constantinople. The artificial character however of his writings indicates the decadence of literary power; he could skillfully imitate the style of ancient writers, but he could not inform himself with their spirit; "his productions" says Gibbon [Ch. xxiv], "are for the most part the vain and idle composition of an orator who cultivated the science of words."

In the school of Libanius Chrysostom no doubt studied the best classical Greek authors, and although he retained little admiration for them in later life and probably read them but rarely, his tenacious memory enabled him to the last to adorn his homilies with quotations from Homer, Plato and the Tragedians. In the school of Libanius also he began to practice his nascent power of eloquence, and a speech which he made in honor of the emperors is highly commended in an extant letter of his master. Thus, the Pagan sophist helped to forge the weapons which were destined to be turned against his own cause. When he was on his deathbed being asked by his friends who was most worthy to succeed him, "it would have been John," he replied, "if the Christians had not stolen him from us."

In due time Chrysostom began to practice as a lawyer; and as the profession of the law was reckoned one of the surest avenues to political distinction for a man of talent, and the speeches of Chrysostom excited great admiration, a brilliant and prosperous career seemed to lie before him. But the soul of the young advocate had drunk draughts from a purer wellspring than the school of Libanius could supply, and like many other Christians in that age when society, even Christian society, was deeply tainted by Pagan sentiments and habits of life, especially in a profligate city like Antioch, he recoiled from the contrast between the morality of the world in which he lived, and the standard of holiness which was presented in the Gospel. The chicanery and rapacity also prevalent in the profession which he had adopted became especially repugnant to his conscience. And these feelings were strengthened by the influence of his intimate friend Basil who had been a fellow pupil with him at the school of Libanius.

The first book of the treatise on the Priesthood opens with a description of his friendship with Basil; how they studied the same subjects together under the same teachers, and how entirely harmonious they were in all their tastes, and inclinations [ci and ii.] Nevertheless, when Basil decided to follow what

Chrysostom calls the "true philosophy," by which he means a life of religious seclusion and study, Chrysostom could not immediately make up his mind to follow his example. The balance he says was no longer even between them; the scale of Basil mounted heavenward, while his own was depressed by the weight of earthly interests, and youthful ambitions. For a time, he continued to practice in the law courts and to frequent the theatre, and other places of amusement. But gradually the study of Scripture, and saintly Bishop of Antioch so wrought upon his mind that he resolved to abandon his secular calling. And in the first place after the usual course of probation he was baptized. It may seem surprising that he had not been baptized in childhood; but a corrupt practice of delaying baptism (which Chrysostom himself often reprobates in his Homilies) was prevalent at that time. It was due in some persons to a notion that sin before Baptism was comparatively venial, in others to a dread of binding themselves or their children to the purity of life which was demanded by the Baptismal vows. In the case of Chrysostom it is possible, I think, that the distracted condition of the church in Antioch may have operated as a reason, perhaps the chief reason for the delay. At the date of his birth (about A.D. 345) and for sixteen years afterwards the See was occupied by Arian Bishops of the most worldly time-serving type. The good Catholic Bishop Meletius was appointed in 361 and it was probably some seven or eight years later that Chrysostom was baptized by him and ordained to the office of Reader in the Church.

There can be no doubt that Baptism, from

whatever cause delayed, must have come home to the recipient at last with all the more solemnity of meaning. It was often a decisive turning point in the life, the beginning of a definite renunciation of the world, and dedication of the whole man to God. To Chrysostom it evidently was this. For a time, he became an enthusiastic ascetic; and then settled down into that more tranquil, but intense glow of piety which burned with unabated force to the close of his life. His baptism and the relinquishment of his secular calling are probably alluded to in the following treatise c. 3. where he speaks of "emerging a little from the flood of worldliness" in which he had been involved. His friend Basil who received him with open arms does not seem to have joined any monastic community, but merely to have been living in retirement and practicing some of the usual monastic austerities. The two friends now formed a plan for withdrawing together to some quiet retreat, there to support one another in habits of study, meditation, and prayer. c. 4. The execution of the project was delayed for a time by the passionate entreaties of Chrysostom's mother that he would not deprive her of his companionship and protection. c. 5. He must have been a poor companion however, for we learn (vi. c. 12) that he rarely went outside the house, maintained an almost perpetual silence, and was constantly absorbed in study and prayer. He and Basil in fact formed with a few other friends a voluntary association of youthful ascetics who lived under a strict rule. We might compare it with the association or club formed by John Wesley and his brother at Oxford which first earned for them the nickname of

"Methodists." Chrysostom and his friends placed the general regulation of their studies and religious life under Diodorus and Carterius, the presidents of the two principal monastic communities in the neighborhood of Antioch. Diodorus was a man of learning and ability, opposed to those mystical and allegorical interpretations of Holy Scripture which often disguised rather than elucidated the real meaning of the sacred text, so that to his training probably we are largely indebted for that clear, sensible practical method of exposition in which Chrysostom so remarkably excels nearly all the ancient father of the Church.

Not long after the two friends had adopted this course of life, probably about the year 374, they were agitated by a report that they were likely to be advanced to the Episcopate (c. 6.) By a custom which was then common in the Church they were liable if elected by the clergy and people to be forcibly seized and ordained however unwilling they might be to accept the dignity [see notes to chapters 6 and 7]. Basil entreated his friend that in this crisis of their lives they might act as in former times in concert, and together accept, or evade, if possible, the expected but unwelcome honor. Chrysostom affected assent to this proposal, but secretly resolved to entrap Basil into the sacred office for which he considered him to be as eminently fitted as he deemed himself to be unworthy. The Church should not on account of his own feebleness be deprived if he could help it, of the able ministrations of such a man as Basil. Accordingly, when some agents of the electing body [as to the composition of this body, see note 3, p. 21] were sent to seize the two young men, Chrysostom contrived to hide himself. His language c. 6. seems to imply that he had some intimation of their coming which he purposely withheld from Basil who consequently was caught. He made at first a violent resistance, but the officials led him to suppose that Chrysostom had already submitted, and under this delusion he acquiesced. When he discovered the trick which had been played upon him, he naturally reproached Chrysostom bitterly for his unkind treachery. But the conscience of Chrysostom seems to have been quite at ease throughout the transaction. He regarded it as a pious fraud and when he saw the mingled distress and anger of his friend he could not refrain, he says, from laughing aloud for joy, and thanking God for the success of his stratagem. The remainder of the 1st Book [chs. 8, 9] is occupied by Chrysostom's vindication of his conduct, the principle that deceit for a righteous end is often salutary and justifiable being maintained with an ingenuity and skill which bespeaks a man who had recently practiced in the law courts. His arguments indeed savor somewhat unpleasantly of casuistry, and it must be confessed that in his conduct on this occasion there is a tinge of something like oriental duplicity which is repugnant to our moral sense. On the other hand it must be borne in mind that neither in the East nor in the West, for many ages were "pious frauds" absolutely condemned by the conscience of Christendom; there was always an inclination to judge each case on its own merits, and to condone if not to approve those in which the balance of evidence was in favor of a righteous or holy purpose, and a beneficial result. And it must also be owned, in justice to Chrysostom, that one of the qualities most conspicuous in him throughout the whole of his subsequent career is fearless, straightforward honesty alike in act and in speech; and this under the pressure very often of strong temptation to dissemble and temporize.

The remaining books on the Priesthood treat of the pre-eminent dignity, and sanctity of the priestly office and the peculiar difficulties and perils which beset it. They abound with wise and weighty observations instructive for all times, but they are also interesting from the light which they throw upon the condition of the Church and of society in the age when Chrysostom lived. It is to be noted that he is speaking of the priesthood generally and that it is not always easy to say in any given passage which of the first two orders in the ministry he has in his mind. In many instances perhaps he was not thinking of one more than the other. Where, as was very commonly the case, the jurisdiction of a bishop did not extend very far beyond the limits of the city in which his See was placed, his functions would more nearly resemble those which in our day are discharged by the incumbent of a large town parish than those which are performed by the modern Bishop of a large diocese. He was the chief pastor of the people, as well as the overseer of the clergy. Chrysostom's friend Basil has been confused by some with the great Basil, Bishop of Cæsarea in Cappadocia, who was fifteen years older than Chrysostom, by others with Basil Bishop of Seleucia, who was many years younger. Nothing in fact is known about him beyond what is recorded in this treatise, but he has been conjecturally identified with Basil Bishop of Raphnea in Syria, not far from Antioch, who attended the Council of Constantinople in 381.

TREATISE ON THE PRIESTHOOD.

Book I.

1. I had many genuine and true friends, men who understood the laws of friendship, and faithfully observed them; but out of this large number there was one who excelled all the rest in his attachment to me, striving to outstrip them as much as they themselves outstripped ordinary acquaintance. He was one of those who were constantly at my side; for we were engaged in the same studies and employed the same teachers. We had the same eagerness and zeal about the studies at which we worked, and a passionate desire produced by the same circumstances was equally strong in both of us. For not only when we were attending school, but after we had left it, when it became necessary to consider what course of life it would be best for us to adopt, we found ourselves to be of the same mind.

2. And in addition to these, there were other things also which preserved and maintained this concord unbroken and secure. For as regarded the greatness of our fatherland neither had one cause to vaunt himself over the other, nor was I burdened with riches, and he pinched by poverty, but our means corresponded as closely as our tastes. Our families also were of equal rank, and thus everything concurred with our disposition.

3. But when it became our duty to pursue the blessed life of monks, and the true philosophy, our balance was no longer even, but his scale mounted high, while I, still entangled in the lusts of this world, dragged mine down and kept it low, weighting it with those fancies in which youths are apt to indulge. For the future

our friendship indeed remained as firm as it was before, but our intercourse was interrupted; for it was impossible for persons who were not interested about the same things to spend much time together. But as soon as I also began to emerge a little from the flood of worldliness, he received me with open arms; yet not even thus could we maintain our former equality: for having got the start of me in time, and having displayed great earnestness, he rose again above my level, and soared to a great height.

4. Being a good man, however, and placing a high value on my friendship, he separated himself from all the rest (of the brethren), and spent the whole of his time with me, which he had desired to do before, but had been prevented as I was saying by my frivolity. For it was impossible for a man who attended the law-courts and was in a flutter of excitement about the pleasures of the stage, to be often in the company of one who was nailed to his books, and never set foot in the marketplace. Consequently, when the hindrances were removed, and he had brought me into the same condition of life as himself, he gave free vent to the desire with which he had long been laboring. He could not bear leaving me even for a moment, and he persistently urged that we should each of us abandon our own home and share a common dwelling: —in fact he persuaded me, and the affair was taken in hand.

5. But the continual lamentations of my mother hindered me from granting him the favor, or rather from receiving this boon at his hands. For when she perceived that I was meditating this step, she took me into her own private chamber, and, sitting near me on the bed where she had given birth to me, she shed torrents of tears, to which she added words yet more pitiable than her

weeping, in the following lamentable strain: My child, it was not the will of Heaven that I should long enjoy the benefit of thy father's virtue. For his death soon followed the pangs which I endured at thy birth, leaving you an orphan and me a widow before my time to face all the horrors of widowhood, which only those who have experienced them can fairly understand. For no words are adequate to describe the tempest tossed condition of a young woman who, having but lately left her paternal home, and being inexperienced in business, is suddenly racked by an overwhelming sorrow, and compelled to support a load of care too great for her age and sex. For she has to correct the laziness of servants, and to be on the watch for their rogueries, to repel the designs of relations, to bear bravely the threats of those who collect the public taxes, and harshness in the imposition of rates. And if the departed one should have left a child, even if it be a girl, great anxiety will be caused to the mother, although free from much expense and fear: but a boy fills her with ten thousand alarms and many anxieties every day, to say nothing of the great expense which one is compelled to incur if she wishes to bring him up in a liberal way. None of these things, however, induced me to enter into a second marriage, or introduce a second husband into thy father's house: but I held on as I was, in the midst of the storm and uproar, and did not shun the iron furnace of widowhood. My foremost help indeed was the grace from above; but it was no small consolation to me under those terrible trials to look continually on thy face and to preserve in you a living image of him who had gone, an image indeed which was a fairly exact likeness.

On this account, even when you were an infant, and had not yet learned to speak, a time when children are the greatest delight to their parents, you didst afford me much comfort. Nor indeed can you complain that, although I bore my widowhood bravely, I diminished thy patrimony, which I know has been the fate of many who have had the misfortune to be orphans. For, besides keeping the whole of it intact, I spared no expense which was needful to give you an honorable position, spending for this purpose some of my own fortune, and of my marriage dowry. Yet do not think that I say these things by way of reproaching you; only in return for all these benefits I beg one favor: do not plunge me into a second widowhood; nor revive the grief which is now laid to rest: wait for my death: it may be in a little while I shall depart. The young indeed look forward to a distant old age; but we who have grown old have nothing but death to wait for. When then, you shall have committed my body to the ground, and mingled my bones with thy father's, embark for a long voyage, and set sail on any sea you wilt then there will be no one to hinder you: but as long as my life lasts, be content to live with me. Do not, I pray you, oppose God in vain, involving me without cause, who have done you no wrong, in these great calamities. For if you have any reason to complain that I drag you into worldly cares, and force you to attend to business, do not be restrained by any reverence for the laws of nature, for training or custom, but fly from me as an enemy; but if, on the contrary, I do everything to provide leisure for thy journey through this life, let this bond at least if nothing else keep you by me. For could you say that ten thousand loved you, yet no one will afford you the enjoyment of so much liberty, seeing there is no one who is equally anxious for thy welfare.

6. These words, and more, my mother spoke to

me, and I related them to that noble youth. But he, so far from being disheartened by these speeches, was the more urgent in making the same request as before. Now while we were thus situated, he continually entreating, and I refusing my assent, we were both of us disturbed by a report suddenly reaching us that we were about to be advanced to the dignity of the episcopate. As soon as I heard this rumor I was seized with alarm and perplexity: with alarm lest I should be made captive against my will, and perplexity, inquiring as I often did whence any such idea concerning us could have entered the minds of these men; for looking to myself I found nothing worthy of such an honor. But that noble youth having come to me privately, and having conferred with me about these things as if with one who was ignorant of the rumor, begged that we might in this instance also as formerly shape our action and our counsels the same way: for he would readily follow me whichever course I might pursue, whether I attempted flight or submitted to be captured. Perceiving then his eagerness, and considering that I should inflict a loss upon the whole body of the Church if, owing to my own weakness, I were to deprive the flock of Christ of a young man who was so good and so well qualified for the supervision of large numbers, I abstained from disclosing to him the purpose which I had formed, although I had never before allowed any of my plans to be concealed from him. I now told him that it would be best to postpone our decision concerning this matter to another season, as it was not immediately pressing, and by so doing persuaded him to dismiss it from his thoughts, and at the same time encouraged him to hope that, if such a thing should ever happen to us, I should be of the same mind with him. But after a short time, when one who was to ordain us arrived, I kept myself concealed, but Basil, ignorant of this, was taken away on another pretext, and made to take the yoke, hoping from the promises which I had made to him that I should certainly follow, or rather supposing that he was following me. For some of those who were present, seeing that he resented being seized, deceived him by exclaiming how strange it was that one who was generally reputed to be the more hot tempered (meaning me), had yielded very mildly to the judgment of the Fathers, whereas he, who was reckoned a much wiser and milder kind of man, had shown himself hotheaded and conceited, being unruly, restive, and contradictory. Having yielded to these remonstrances, and afterwards having learned that I had escaped capture, he came to me in deep dejection, sat down near me and tried to speak, but was hindered by distress of mind and inability to express in words the violence to which he had been subjected. No sooner had he opened his mouth than he was prevented from utterance by grief cutting short his words before they could pass his lips. Seeing, then, his tearful and agitated condition, and knowing as I did the cause, I laughed for joy, and, seizing his right hand, I forced a kiss on him, and praised God that my plan had ended so successfully, as I had always prayed it might. But when he saw that I was delighted and beaming with joy, and understood that he had been deceived by me, he was yet more vexed and distressed.

7. And when he had a little recovered from this agitation of mind, he began: If you have rejected the part allotted to you, and have no further regard for me (I know not indeed for what cause), you ought at least to consider your own reputation; but as it is you have opened the

mouths of all, and the world is saying that you have declined this ministry through love of vainglory, and there is no one who will deliver you from this accusation. As for me, I cannot bear to go into the marketplace; there are so many who come up to me and reproach me every day. For, when they see me anywhere in the city, all my intimate friends take me aside, and cast the greater part of the blame upon me. Knowing his intention, they say, for none of his affairs could be kept secret from you, you should not have concealed it, but ought to have communicated it to us, and we should have been at no loss to devise some plan for capturing him. But I am too much ashamed and abashed to tell them that I did not know you had long been plotting this trick, lest they should say that our friendship was a mere pretense. For even if it is so, as indeed it is—nor would you yourself deny it after what you have done to me—yet it is well to hide our misfortune from the outside world, and persons who entertain but a moderate opinion of us. I shrink from telling them the truth, and how things really stand with us, and I am compelled in future to keep silence, and look down on the ground, and turn away to avoid those whom I meet. For if I escape the condemnation on the former charge, I am forced to undergo judgment for speaking falsehood. For they will never believe me when I say that you ranged Basil amongst those who are not permitted to know your secret affairs. Of this, however, I will not take much account, since it has seemed agreeable to you, but how shall we endure the future disgrace? for some accuse you of arrogance, others of vainglory: while those who are our more merciful accusers, lay both these offences to our charge, and add that we have insulted those who did us honor, although had they experienced even greater indignity it would only have served them right for passing over so many and such distinguished men and advancing mere youths, who were but yesterday immersed in the interests of this world, to such a dignity as they never have dreamed of obtaining, in order that they may for a brief season knit the eyebrows, wear dusky garments, and put on a grave face. Those who from the dawn of manhood to extreme old age have diligently practiced self-discipline, are now to be placed under the government of youths who have not even heard the laws which should regulate their administration of this office. I am perpetually assailed by persons who say such things and worse, and am at a loss how to reply to them; but I pray you tell me: for I do not suppose that you took to flight and incurred such hatred from such distinguished men without cause or consideration, but that your decision was made with reasoning and circumspection: whence also I conjecture that you have some argument ready for your defense. Tell me, then, whether there is any fair excuse which I can make to those who accuse us.

For I do not demand any account for the wrongs which I have sustained at your hands, nor for the deceit or treachery you have practiced, nor for the advantage which you have derived from me in the past. For I placed my very life, so to say, in your hands, yet you have treated me with as much guile as if it had been your business to guard yourself against an enemy. Yet if you knew this decision of ours to be profitable, you ought not to have avoided the gain: if on the contrary injurious, you should have saved me also from the loss, as you always said that you esteemed me before everyone else. But you have done everything to make me fall into the snare: and you had no need of guile and hypocrisy in dealing with one who was wont to display the utmost sincerity and candor in speech and action towards you. Nevertheless, as I said, I do not now accuse you of any of these things, or reproach you for the lonely position in which you have placed me by breaking off those conferences from which we often derived no small pleasure and profit; but all these things I pass by, and bear in silence and meekness, not that you hast acted meekly in transgressing against me, but because from the day that I cherished thy friendship I laid it down as a rule for myself, that whatever sorrow you might cause me I would never force you to the necessity of an apology. For you know yourself that you have inflicted no small loss on me if at least you remember what we were always saying ourselves, and the outside world also said concerning us, that it was a great gain for us to be of one mind and be guarded by each other's friendship. Everyone said, indeed, that our concord would bring no small advantage to many besides ourselves; I never perceived, however, so far as I am concerned, how it could be of advantage to others: but I did say that we should at least derive this benefit from it: that those who wished to contend with us would find us difficult to master. And I never ceased reminding you of these things: saying the age is a cruel one, and designing men are many, genuine love is no more, and the deadly pest of envy has crept into its place: we walk in the midst of snares, and on the edge of battlements; those who are ready to rejoice in our misfortunes, if any should befall us, are many and beset us from many quarters: whereas there is no one to condole with us, or at least the number of such may be easily counted. Beware that we do not by separation incur much ridicule, and damage worse than ridicule. Brother aided by brother is like a strong city and a well-fortified kingdom. Do not dissolve this genuine intimacy, nor break down the fortress. Such things and more I was continually saying, not indeed that I ever suspected anything of this kind, but supposing you to be entirely sound in your relation towards me, I did it as a superfluous precaution, wishing to preserve in health one who was already sound; but unwittingly, as it seems, I was administering medicines to a sick man: and even so, I have not been fortunate enough to do any good, and have gained nothing by my excess of forethought. For having totally cast away all these considerations, without giving them a thought, you have turned me adrift like an unballasted vessel on an untried ocean, taking no heed of those fierce billows which, I must encounter. For if it should ever be my lot to undergo calumny, or mockery, or any other kind of insult or menace (and such things must frequently occur), to whom shall I fly for refuge: to whom shall I impart my distress, who will be willing to succor me and drive back my assailants and put a stop to their assaults? who will solace me and prepare me to bear the coarse ribaldry which may yet be in store for me? There is no one since you stand aloof from this terrible strife and cannot even hear my cry. Sees you then what mischief you hast wrought? now that you hast dealt the blow, dost you perceive what a deadly wound you hast inflicted? But let all this pass: for it is impossible to undo the past, or to find a path through pathless difficulties. What shall I say to the outside world? what defense shall I make to their accusations?

8. Chrysostom: Be of good cheer, I replied, for I am not only ready to answer for myself in these matters, but I will also endeavor as well as I am able to render an account of those for which you have not held me

answerable. Indeed, if you wish it, I will make them the starting point of my defense. For it would be a strange piece of stupidity on my part if, thinking only of praise from the outside public, and doing my best to silence their accusations, I were unable to convince my dearest of all friends that I am not wronging him, and were to treat him with indifference greater than the zeal which he has displayed on my behalf, treating me with such forbearance as even to refrain from accusing me of the wrongs which he says he has suffered from me, and putting his own interests out of the question in consideration for mine.

What is the wrong that I have done you since I have determined to embark from this point upon the sea of apology? Is it that I misled you and concealed my purpose? Yet I did it for the benefit of thyself who was deceived, and of those to whom I surrendered you by means of this deceit. For if the evil of deception is absolute, and it is never right to make use of it, I am prepared to pay any penalty you please: or rather, as you will never endure to inflict punishment upon me, I shall subject myself to the same condemnation which is pronounced by judges on evil-doers when their accusers have convicted them. But if the thing is not always harmful, but becomes good or bad according to the intention of those who practice it, you must desist from complaining of deceit, and prove that it has been devised against you for a bad purpose; and as long as this proof is wanting it would only be fair for those who wish to conduct themselves prudently, not only to abstain from reproaches and accusation, but even to give a friendly reception to the deceiver. For a well-timed deception, undertaken with an upright intention, has such advantages, that many persons have often had to undergo punishment for abstaining from fraud. And if you investigate the history of generals who have enjoyed the highest reputation from the earliest ages, you will find that most of their triumphs were achieved by stratagem, and that such are more highly commended than those who conquer in open fight. For the latter conduct their campaigns with greater expenditure of money and men, so that they gain nothing by the victory, but suffer just as much distress as those who have been defeated, both in the sacrifice of troops and the exhaustion of funds. But, besides this, they are not even permitted to enjoy all the glory which pertains to the victory; for no small part of it is reaped by those who have fallen, because in spirit they were victorious, their defeat was only a bodily one: so that had it been possible for them not to fall when they were wounded, and death had not come and put the finishing stroke to their labors, there would have been no end of their prowess. But one who has been able to gain the victory by stratagem involves the enemy in ridicule as well as disaster. Again, in the other case both sides equally carry off the honors bestowed upon valor, whereas in this case they do not equally obtain those which are bestowed on wisdom, but the prize falls entirely to the victors, and, another point no less important is that they preserve the joy of the victory for the state unalloyed; for abundance of resources and multitudes of men are not like mental powers: the former indeed if continually used in war necessarily become exhausted, and fail those who possess them, whereas it is the nature of wisdom to increase the more it is exercised. And not in war only, but also in peace the need of deceit may be found, not merely in reference to the affairs of the state, but also in private life, in the dealings of husband with wife and wife with husband, son with father, friend with friend, and also children with a parent. For the daughter of Saul would not have been able to rescue her husband out of Saul's hands except by deceiving her father. And her brother, wishing to save him whom she had rescued when he was again in danger, made use of the same weapon as the wife.

Basil: But none of these cases apply to me: for I am not an enemy, nor one of those who are striving to injure you, but quite the contrary. For I entrusted all my interests to your judgment, and always followed it whenever you bid me.

Chrysostom: But, my admirable and excellent Sir, this is the very reason why I took the precaution of saying that it was a good thing to employ this kind of deceit, not only in war, and in dealing with enemies, but also in peace, and in dealing with our dearest friends. For as a proof that it is beneficial not only to the deceivers, but also to those who are deceived; if you go to any of the physicians and ask them how they relieve their patients from disease, they will tell you that they do not depend upon their professional skill alone, but sometimes conduct the sick to health by availing themselves of deceit, and blending the assistance which they derive from it with their art. For when the waywardness of the patient and the obstinacy of the complaint baffle the counsels of the physicians, it is then necessary to put on the mask of deceit in order that, as on the stage, they may be able to hide what really takes place. But, if you please, I will relate to you one instance of stratagem out of many which I have heard of being contrived by the sons of the healing art. A man was once suddenly attacked by a fever of great severity; the burning heat increased, and the patient rejected the remedies which could have reduced it and craved for a draught of pure wine, passionately entreating all who approached to give it him and enable him to satiate this deadly craving—I say deadly, for if anyone had gratified this request he would not only have exasperated the fever, but also have driven the unhappy man frantic. Thereupon, professional skill being baffled, and at the end of its resources and utterly thrown away, stratagem stepped in and displayed its power in the way which I will now relate. For the physician took an earthen cup brought straight out of the furnace, and having steeped it in wine, then drew it out empty, filled it with water, and, having ordered the chamber where the sick man lay to be darkened with curtains that the light might not reveal the trick, he gave it him to drink, pretending that it was filled with undiluted wine. And the man, before he had taken it in his hands, being deceived by the smell, did not wait to examine what was given him, but convinced by the odor, and deceived by the darkness, eagerly gulped down the draught, and being satiated with it immediately shook off the feeling of suffocation and escaped the imminent peril. Do you see the advantage of deceit? And if anyone were to reckon up all the tricks of physicians the list would run on to an indefinite length. And not only those who heal the body but those also who attend to the diseases of the soul may be found continually making use of this remedy. Thus, the blessed Paul attracted those multitudes of Jews: with this purpose he circumcised Timothy, although he warned the Galatians in his letter that Christ would not profit those who were circumcised. For this cause he submitted to the law, although he reckoned the righteousness which came from the law but loss after receiving the faith in Christ. For great is the value of deceit, provided it be not introduced with a mischievous intention. In fact, action of this kind ought not to be called deceit, but rather a kind of good management, cleverness and skill, capable of finding out ways where resources fail, and making up for the defects of the mind. For I would not call Phinees a murderer, although he slew two human beings with one stroke: nor yet Elias after the slaughter of the 100 soldiers, and the captain, and the torrents of blood which he caused to be shed by the destruction of those who sacrificed to devils. For if we were to concede this, and to examine the bare deeds in themselves apart from the intention of the doers, one might if he pleased judge Abraham guilty of child-murder and accuse his grandson and descendant of wickedness and guile. For the one got possession of the birthright, and the other transferred the wealth of the Egyptians to the host of the Israelites. But this is not the case: away with the audacious thought! For we not only acquit them of blame, but also admire them because of these things, since even God commended them for the same. For that man would fairly deserve to be called a deceiver who made an unrighteous use of the practice, not one who did so with a salutary purpose. And often it is necessary to deceive, and to do the greatest benefits by means of this device, whereas he who has gone by a straight course has done great mischief to the person whom he has not deceived.

Book II.

1. That it is possible then to make use of deceit for a good purpose, or rather that in such a case it ought not

to be called deceit, but a kind of good management worthy of all admiration, might be proved at greater length; but since what has already been said suffices for demonstration, it would be irksome and tedious to lengthen out my discourse upon the subject. And now it will remain for you to prove whether I have not employed this art to your advantage.

Basil: And what kind of advantage have I derived from this piece of good management, or wise policy, or whatever you may please to call it, so as to persuade me that I have not been deceived by you?

Chrysostom: What advantage, pray, could be greater than to be seen doing those things which Christ with his own lips declared to be proofs of love to Himself? For addressing the leader of the apostles, He said, "Peter, loves you me?" and when he confessed that he did, the Lord added, "if you love me tend my sheep." The Master asked the disciple if He was loved by him, not in order to get information (how should He who penetrates the hearts of all men?), but in order to teach us how great an interest He takes in the superintendence of these sheep. This being plain, it will likewise be manifest that a great and unspeakable reward will be reserved for him whose labors are concerned with these sheep, upon which Christ places such a high value. For when we see any one bestowing care upon members of our household, or upon our flocks, we count his zeal for them as a sign of love towards ourselves: yet all these things are to be bought for money:—with how great a gift then will He requite those who tend the flock which He purchased, not with money, nor anything of that kind, but by His own death, giving his own blood as the price of the herd. Wherefore when the disciple said, "You knows Lord that

I love You," and invoked the beloved one Himself as a witness of his love, the Savior did not stop there, but added that which was the token of love. For He did not at that time wish to show how much Peter loved Him, but how much He Himself loved His own Church, and he desired to teach Peter and all of us that we also should bestow much zeal upon the same. For why did God not spare His only begotten Son, but delivered Him up, although the only one He had? It was that He might reconcile to Himself those who were disposed towards Him as enemies and make them His peculiar people. For what purpose did He shed His blood? It was that He might win these sheep which He entrusted to Peter and his successors. Naturally then did Christ say, "Who then is the faithful and wise servant, whom his lord shall make ruler over His household." Again, the words are those of one who is in doubt, yet the speaker did not utter them in doubt, but just as He asked Peter whether he loved Him, not from any need to learn the affection of the disciple, but from a desire to show the exceeding depth of his own love: so now also when He says, "Who then is the faithful and wise servant?" he speaks not as being ignorant who is faithful and wise, but as desiring to set forth the rarity of such a character, and the greatness of this office. Observe at any rate how great the reward is— "He will appoint him," he says, "ruler over all his goods."

2. Will you, then, still contend that you were not rightly deceived, when you are about to superintend the things which belong to God, and are doing that which when Peter did the Lord said he should be able to surpass the rest of the apostles, for His words were, "Peter, loves you me more than these?" Yet He might have said to him, "If you love me practice fasting, sleeping on the ground,

and prolonged vigils, defend the wronged, be as a father to orphans, and supply the place of a husband to their mother." But as a matter of fact, setting aside all these things, what does He say? "Tend my sheep." For those things which I have already mentioned might easily be performed by many even of those who are under authority, women as well as men; but when one is required to preside over the Church, and to be entrusted with the care of so many souls, the whole female sex must retire before the magnitude of the task, and the majority of men also; and we must bring forward those who to a large extent surpass all others, and soar as much above them in excellence of spirit as Saul overtopped the whole Hebrew nation in bodily stature: or rather far more. For in this case let me not take the height of shoulders as the standard of inquiry; but let the distinction between the pastor and his charge be as great as that between rational man and irrational creatures, not to say even greater, inasmuch as the risk is concerned with things of far greater importance. He indeed who has lost sheep, either through the ravages of wolves, or the attacks of robbers, or through murrain, or any other disaster befalling them, might perhaps obtain some indulgence from the owner of the flock; and even if the latter should demand satisfaction the penalty would be only a matter of money: but he who has human beings entrusted to him, the rational flock of Christ, incurs a penalty in the first place for the loss of the sheep, which goes beyond material things and touches his own life: and in the second place he has to carry on a far greater and more difficult contest. For he has not to contend with wolves, nor to dread robbers, nor to consider how he may avert pestilence from the flock. With whom then has he to fight? with whom has he to wrestle? Listen to the words of St. Paul. "We wrestle not against flesh and blood, but against principalities, against powers, against the rulers of the darkness of this world, against spiritual wickedness in high places." Do you see the terrible multitude of enemies, and their fierce squadrons, not steel clad, but endued with a nature which is of itself an equivalent for a complete suit of armor. Would you see yet another host, stern and cruel, beleaguering this flock? This also you shall behold from the same post of observation. For he who has discoursed to us concerning the others, points out these enemies also to us, speaking in a certain place on this wise: "The works of the flesh are manifest, which are these, fornication, adultery, uncleanness, lasciviousness, idolatry, witchcraft, hatred, variance, emulation, wrath, strife, backbiting, whisperings, swellings, tumults," and many more besides; for he did not make a complete list, but left us to understand the rest from these. Moreover, in the case of the shepherd of irrational creatures, those who wish to destroy the flock, when they see the guardian take to flight, cease making war upon him, and are contented with the seizure of the cattle: but in this case, even should they capture the whole flock, they do not leave the shepherd unmolested, but attack him all the more, and wax bolder, ceasing not until they have either overthrown him, or have themselves been vanquished. Again, the afflictions of sheep are manifest, whether it be famine, or pestilence, or wounds, or whatsoever else it may be which distresses them, and this might help not a little towards the relief of those who are oppressed in these ways. And there is yet another fact greater than this which facilitates release from this kind of infirmity. And what is that? The shepherds with great authority compel the sheep to receive the remedy when they do not willingly submit to it. For it is easy to bind them when cautery or cutting is required, and to keep them inside the fold for a long time, whenever it is expedient, and to bring them one kind of food instead of another, and to cut them off from their supplies of water, and all other things which the shepherds may decide to be conducive to their health they perform with great ease.

3. But in the case of human infirmities, it is not easy in the first place for a man to discern them, for no man "knows the things of a man, save the spirit of man which is in him." How then can anyone apply the remedy for the disease of which he does not know the character, often indeed being unable to understand it even should he happen to sicken with it himself? And even when it becomes manifest, it causes him yet more trouble: for it is not possible to doctor all men with the same authority with which the shepherd treats his sheep. For in this case also it is necessary to bind and to restrain from food, and to use cautery or the knife: but the reception of the treatment depends on the will of the patient, not of him who applies the remedy. For this also was perceived by that wonderful man (St. Paul) when he said to the Corinthians— "Not for that we have dominion over your faith but are helpers of your joy." For Christians above all men are not permitted forcibly to correct the failings of those who sin. Secular judges indeed, when they have captured malefactors under the law, show their authority to be great, and prevent them even against their will from following their own devices: but in our case the wrong doer must be made better, not by force, but by persuasion. For neither has authority of this kind for the restraint of sinners been given us by law, nor, if it had been given,

should we have any field for the exercise of our power, inasmuch as God rewards those who abstain from evil by their own choice, not of necessity. Consequently, much skill is required that our patients may be induced to submit willingly to the treatment prescribed by the physicians, and not only this, but that they may be grateful also for the cure. For if any one when he is bound becomes restive (which it is in his power to be), he makes the mischief worse; and if he should pay no heed to the words which cut like steel, he inflicts another wound by means of this contempt, and the intention to heal only becomes the occasion of a worse disorder. For it is not possible for anyone to cure a man by compulsion against his will.

4. What then is one to do? For if you deal too gently with him who needs a severe application of the knife, and do not strike deep into one who requires such treatment, you remove one part of the sore but leave the other: and if on the other hand you make the requisite incision unsparingly, the patient, driven to desperation by his sufferings, will often fling everything away at once, both the remedy and the bandage, and throw himself down headlong, "breaking the yoke and bursting the band." I could tell of many who have run into extreme evils because the due penalty of their sins was exacted. For we ought not, in applying punishment, merely to proportion it to the scale of the offence, but rather to keep in view the disposition of the sinner, lest whilst wishing to mend what is torn, you make the rent worse, and in your zealous endeavors to restore what is fallen, you make the ruin greater. For weak and careless characters, addicted for the most part to the pleasures of the world, and having occasion to be proud on account of birth and position,

may yet, if gently and gradually brought to repent of their errors, be delivered, partially at least, if not perfectly, from the evils by which they are possessed: but if any one were to inflict the discipline all at once, he would deprive them of this slight chance of amendment. For when once the soul has been forced to put off shame it lapses into a callous condition, and neither yields to kindly words nor bends to threats, nor is susceptible of gratitude, but becomes far worse than that city which the prophet reproached, saying, "you has the face of a harlot, refusing to be ashamed before all men." Therefore, the pastor has need of much discretion, and of a myriad eyes to observe on every side the habit of the soul. For as many are uplifted to pride, and then sink into despair of their salvation, from inability to endure severe remedies, so are there some, who from paying no penalty equivalent to their sins, fall into negligence, and become far worse, and are impelled to greater sins. It behooves the priest therefore to leave none of these things unexamined, but, after a thorough inquiry into all of them, to apply such remedies as he has appositely to each case, lest his zeal prove to be in vain. And not in this matter only, but also in the work of knitting together the severed members of the Church, one can see that he has much to do. For the pastor of sheep has his flock following him, wherever he may lead them: and if any should stray out of the straight path, and, deserting the good pasture, feed in unproductive or rugged places, a loud shout suffices to collect them and bring back to the fold those who have been parted from it: but if a human being wanders away from the right faith, great exertion, perseverance and patience are required; for he cannot be dragged back by force, nor constrained by fear, but must be led back by persuasion to the truth from which he originally swerved. The pastor therefore ought to be of a noble spirit, so as not to despond, or to despair of the salvation of wanderers from the fold, but continually to reason with himself and say, "Peradventure God will give them repentance to the acknowledging of the truth, and that they may recover themselves out of the snare of the devil." Therefore, the Lord, when addressing His disciples, said, "Who then is the faithful and wise servant?" For he indeed who disciplines himself compasses only his own advantage, but the benefit of the pastoral function extends to the whole people. And one who dispenses money to the needy, or otherwise succors the oppressed, benefits his neighbors to some extent, but so much less than the priest in proportion as the body is inferior to the soul. Rightly therefore did the Lord say that zeal for the flock was a token of love for Himself.

Basil: But you thyself—dost you not love Christ?

Chrysostom: Yea, I love Him, and shall never cease loving Him; but I fear lest I should provoke Him whom I love.

Basil: But what riddle can there be more obscure than this—Christ has commanded him who loves Him to tend His sheep, and yet you say that you decline to tend them because you love Him who gave this command?

Chrysostom: My saying is no riddle, but very intelligible and simple, for if I were well qualified to administer this office, as Christ desired it, and then shunned it, my remark might be open to doubt, but since the infirmity of my spirit renders me useless for this ministry, why does my saying deserve to be called in question? For I fear lest if I took the flock in hand when it was in good condition and well nourished, and then wasted it through my unskillfulness, I should provoke against myself the God who so loved the flock as to give Himself up for their salvation and ransom.

Basil: You speak in jest: for if you were in earnest, I know not how you would have proved me to be justly grieved otherwise than by means of these very words whereby you have endeavored to dispel my dejection. I knew indeed before that you had deceived and betrayed me, but much more now, when you have undertaken to clear yourself of my accusations, do I plainly perceive and understand the extent of the evils into which you have led me. For if you withdrew yourself from this ministry because you were conscious that your spirit was not equal to the burden of the task, I ought to have been rescued from it before you, even if I had chanced to have a great desire for it, to say nothing of having confided to you the entire decision of these matters: but as it is, you have looked solely to your own interest and neglected mine. Would indeed you had entirely neglected them; then I should have been well content: but you plotted to facilitate my capture by those who wished to seize me. For you cannot take shelter in the argument that public opinion deceived you and induced you to imagine great and wonderful things concerning me. For I was none of your wonderful and distinguished men, nor, had this been the case, ought you to have preferred public opinion to truth. For if I had never permitted you to enjoy my society, you might have seemed to have a reasonable pretext for being guided in your vote by public report; but if there is no one who has such thorough knowledge of my affairs, if you are acquainted with my character better than my parents and those who brought me up, what argument can you employ which will be convincing enough to persuade your hearers that you did not purposely thrust me into this danger: say, what answer shall I make to your accusers?

Chrysostom: Nay! I will not proceed to those questions until I have resolved such as concern yourself alone, if you were to ask me ten thousand times to dispose of these charges. You said indeed that ignorance would bring me forgiveness, and that I should have been free from all accusation if I had brought you into your present position not knowing anything about you, but that as I did not betray you in ignorance, but was intimately acquainted with your affairs, I was deprived of all reasonable pretext and excuse. But I say precisely the reverse: for in such matters there is need of careful scrutiny, and he who is going to present anyone as qualified for the priesthood ought not to be content with public report only, but should also himself, above all and before all, investigate the man's character. For when the blessed Paul says, "He must also have a good report of them which are without," he does not dispense with an exact and rigorous inquiry, nor does he assign to such testimony precedence over the scrutiny required in such cases. For after much previous discourse, he mentioned this additional testimony, proving that one must not be contented with it alone for elections of this kind, but take it into consideration along with the rest. For public report often speaks false; but when careful investigation precedes, no further danger need be apprehended from it. On this account, after the other kinds of evidence he places that which comes from those who are without. For he did not simply say, "he must have a good report," but added the words, "from them which are without," wishing to show that before the report of those without he must be carefully examined. Inasmuch, then, as I myself knew your affairs better than your parents, as you also yourself acknowledged, I might deserve to be released from all blame. Basil: Nay this is the very reason why you could not escape, if anyone chose to indite you. Do you not remember hearing from me, and often learning from my actual conduct, the feebleness of my character? Were you not perpetually taunting me for my pusillanimity, because I was so easily dejected by ordinary cares? 5. Chrysostom: I do indeed remember often hearing such things said by you; I would not deny it. But if I ever taunted you, I did it in sport and not in serious truth. However, I do not now dispute about these matters, and I claim the same degree of forbearance from you while I wish to make mention of some of the good qualities which you possess. For if you attempt to convict me of saying what is untrue, I shall not spare you, but shall prove that you say these things rather by way of self-depreciation than with a view to truth, and I will employ no evidence but your own words and deeds to demonstrate the truth of my assertion. And now the first question I wish to ask of you is this: do you know how great the power of love is? For omitting all the miracles which were to be wrought by the apostles, Christ said, "Hereby shall men know that ye are my disciples if ye love one another," and Paul said that it was the fulfilling of the law and that in default of it no spiritual gift had any profit. Well, this choice good, the distinguishing mark of Christ's disciples, the gift which is higher than all other gifts, I perceived to be deeply implanted in your soul, and teeming with much fruit. Basil: I acknowledge indeed that the matter is one of deep concern to me, and that I endeavor most earnestly to keep this commandment, but that I have not even half succeeded in so doing, even you yourself would bear me witness if you would leave off talking out of partiality, and simply respect the truth.

6. Chrysostom: Well, then, I shall betake myself to my evidence, and shall now do what I threatened, proving that you wish to disparage yourself rather than to speak the truth. But I will mention a fact which has only just occurred, that no one may suspect me of attempting to obscure the truth by the great lapse of time in relating events long past, as oblivion would then prevent any objection being made to the things which I might say with a view to gratification. For when one of our intimate friends, having been falsely accused of insult and folly, was in extreme peril, you then flung yourself into the midst of the danger, although you were not summoned by anyone, or appealed to by the person who was about to be involved in danger. Such was the fact: but that I may convict you out of your own mouth, I will remind you of the words you uttered: for when some did not approve of this zeal, while others commended and admired it, "How can I help myself?" you said to those who accused you, "for I do not know how otherwise to love than by giving up my life when it is necessary to save any of my friends who is in danger:" thus repeating, in different words, indeed, but with the same meaning, what Christ said to his disciples when he laid down the definition of perfect love. "Greater love," He said, "hath no man than this that a man lay down his life for his friends." If then it is impossible to find greater love than this, you have attained its limit, and both by your deeds and words have crowned the summit. This is why I betrayed you, this is why I contrived that plot. Do I now convince you that it was not from any malicious intent, nor from any desire to thrust

you into danger, but from a persuasion of your future usefulness that I dragged you into this course?

Basil: Do you then suppose that love is sufficient for the correction of one's fellowmen?

Chrysostom: Certainly, it would contribute in a great measure to this end. But if you wish me to produce evidence of your practical wisdom also, I will proceed to do so, and will prove that your understanding exceeds your lovingkindness.

At these remarks he blushed scarlet and said, "Let my character be now dismissed: for it was not about this that I originally demanded an explanation; but if you have any just answer to make to those who are without, I would gladly hear what you have to say. Wherefore, abandoning this vain contest, tell me what defense I shall make, both to those who have honored you and to those who are distressed on their account, considering them to be insulted.

7. Chrysostom: This is just the point to which I am finally hastening, for as my explanation to you has been completed, I shall easily turn to this part of my defense. What then is the accusation made by these persons, and what are their charges? They say that they have been insulted and grievously wronged by me because I have not accepted the honor which they wished to confer upon me. Now in the first place I say that no account should be taken of the insult shown to men, seeing that by paying honor to them I should be compelled to offend God. And I should say to those who are displeased that it is not safe to take offence at these things but does them much harm. For I think that those who stay themselves on God and look to Him alone, ought to be so religiously disposed as not to account such a thing an insult, even if they

happened to be a thousand times dishonored. But that I have not gone so far as even to think of daring anything of this kind is manifest from what I am about to say. For if indeed I had been induced by arrogance and vainglory, as you have often said some slanderously affirm, to assent to my accusers, I should have been one of the most iniquitous of mankind, having treated great and excellent men, my benefactors moreover, with contempt. For if men ought to be punished for wronging those who have never wronged them, how ought we to honor those who have spontaneously preferred to honor us? For no one could possibly say that they were requiting me for any benefits small or great which they had received at my hands. How great a punishment then would one deserve if one requited them in the contrary manner. But if such a thing never entered my mind, and I declined the heavy burden with quite a different intention, why do they refuse to pardon me (even if they do not consent to approve), but accuse me of having selfishly spared my own soul? For so far from having insulted the men in question I should say that I had even honored them by my refusal.

And do not be surprised at the paradoxical nature of my remark, for I shall supply a speedy solution of it.

8. For had I accepted the office, I do not say all men, but those who take pleasure in speaking evil, might have suspected and said many things concerning myself who had been elected and concerning them, the electors: for instance, that they regarded wealth, and admired splendor of rank, or had been induced by flattery to promote me to this honor: indeed I cannot say whether someone might not have suspected that they were bribed by money. Moreover, they would have said, "Christ called fishermen, tentmakers, and publicans to this

dignity, whereas these men reject those who support themselves by daily labor: but if there be anyone who devotes himself to secular learning, and is brought up in idleness, him they receive and admire. For why, pray, have they passed by men who have undergone innumerable toils in the service of the Church, and suddenly dragged into this dignity one who has never experienced any labors of this kind, but has spent all his youth in the vain study of secular learning." These things and more they might have said had I accepted the office: but not so now. For every pretext for maligning is now cut away from them, and they can neither accuse me of flattery, nor the others of receiving bribes, unless some choose to act like mere madmen. For how could one who used flattery and expended money in order to obtain the dignity, have abandoned it to others when he might have obtained it? For this would be just as if a man who had bestowed much labor upon the ground in order that the corn field might be laden with abundant produce, and the presses overflow with wine, after innumerable toils and great expenditure of money were to surrender the fruits to others just when it was time to reap his corn and gather in his vintage. Do you see that although what was said might be far from the truth, nevertheless those who wished to calumniate the electors would then have had a pretext for alleging that the choice was made without fair judgment and consideration. But as it is I have prevented them from being open-mouthed, or even uttering a single word on the subject. Such then and more would have been their remarks at the outset. But after undertaking the ministry I should not have been able day by day to defend myself against accusers, even if I had done everything faultlessly, to say nothing of the many mistakes which I must have made owing to my youth and inexperience. But now I have saved the electors from this kind of accusation also, whereas in the other case I should have involved them in innumerable reproaches. For what would not the world have said? "They have committed affairs of such vast interest and importance to thoughtless youths, they have defiled the flock of God, and Christian affairs have become a jest and a laughing-stock." But now "all iniquity shall stop her mouth." For although they may say these things on your account, you will speedily teach them by your acts that understanding is not to be estimated by age, and the grey head is not to be the test of an elder—that the young man ought not to be absolutely excluded from the ministry, but only the novice: and the difference between the two is great.

Book III.

1. Chrysostom: As regards the insult to those who have done me honor, what I have already said might be sufficient to prove that in avoiding this office I had no desire to put them to shame; but I will now endeavor to make it evident, to the best of my ability, that I was not puffed up by arrogance of any kind. For if the choice of a generalship or a kingdom had been submitted to me, and I had then formed this resolution, anyone might naturally have suspected me of this fault, or rather I should have been found guilty by all men, not of arrogance, but of senseless folly. But when the priesthood is offered to me, which exceeds a kingdom as much as the spirit differs from the flesh, will anyone dare to accuse me of disdain? And is it not preposterous to charge with folly those who reject small things, but when any do this in matters of pre-

eminent importance, to exempt such persons from accusations of mental derangement, and yet subject them to the charge of pride? It is just as if one were to accuse, not of pride, but of insanity, a man who looked with contempt on a herd of oxen and refused to be a herdsman, and yet were to say that a man who declined the empire of the world, and the command of all the armies of the earth, was not mad, but inflated with pride. But this assuredly is not the case; and they who say such things do not injure me more than they injure themselves. For merely to imagine it possible for human nature to despise this dignity is evidence against those who bring this charge of the estimate which they have formed of the office. For if they did not consider it to be an ordinary thing of no great account, such a suspicion as this would never have entered their heads. For why is it that no one has ever dared to entertain such a suspicion with reference to the dignity of the angels, and to say that arrogance is the reason why human nature would not aspire to the rank of the angelic nature? It is because we imagine great things concerning those powers, and this does not suffer us to believe that a man can conceive anything greater than that honor. Wherefore one might with more justice indite those persons of arrogance who accuse me of it. For they would never have suspected this of others if they had not previously depreciated the matter as being of no account. But if they say that I have done this with a view to glory, they will be convicted of fighting openly against themselves and falling into their own snare; for I do not know what kind of arguments they could have sought in preference to these if they had wished to release me from the charge of vainglory.

2. For if this desire had ever entered my mind, I

ought to have accepted the office rather than avoided it. Why? because it would have brought me much glory. For the fact that one of my age, who had so recently abandoned secular pursuits, should suddenly be deemed by all worthy of such admiration as to be advanced to honor before those who have spent all their life in labors of this kind, and to obtain more votes than all of them, might have persuaded all men to anticipate great and marvelous things of me. But, as it is, the greater part of the Church does not know me even by name: so that even my refusal of the office will not be manifest to all, but only to a few, and I am not sure that all even of these know it for certain; but probably many of them either imagine that I was not elected at all, or that I was rejected after the election, being considered unsuitable, not that I avoided the office of my own accord.

3. Basil: But those who do know the truth will be surprised.

Chrysostom: And lo! these are they who, according to you, falsely accuse me of vainglory and pride. Whence then am I to hope for praise? From the many? They do not know the actual fact. From the few? Here again the matter is perverted to my disadvantage. For the only reason why, you have come here now is to learn what answer ought to be given to them. And what shall I now certainly say on account of these things? For wait a little, and you will clearly perceive that even if all know the truth, they ought not to condemn me for pride and love of glory. And in addition to this there is another consideration: that not only those who make this venture, if there be any such (which for my part I do not believe), but also those who suspect it of others, will be involved in no small danger.

4. For the priestly office is indeed discharged on earth, but it ranks amongst heavenly ordinances; and very naturally so: for neither man, nor angel, nor archangel, nor any other created power, but the Paraclete Himself, instituted this vocation, and persuaded men while still abiding in the flesh to represent the ministry of angels. Wherefore the consecrated priest ought to be as pure as if he were standing in the heavens themselves in the midst of those powers. Fearful, indeed, and of most awful import, were the things which were used before the dispensation of grace, as the bells, the pomegranates, the stones on the breastplate and on the ephod, the girdle, the mitre, the long robe, the plate of gold, the holy of holies, the deep silence within. But if anyone should examine the things which belong to the dispensation of grace, he will find that, small as they are, yet are they fearful and full of awe, and that what was spoken concerning the law is true in this case also, that "what has been made glorious hath no glory in this respect by reason of the glory which excellent." For when you see the Lord sacrificed, and laid upon the altar, and the priest standing and praying over the victim, and all the worshippers empurpled with that precious blood, canst you then think that you are still amongst men, and standing upon the earth? Art you not, on the contrary, straightway translated to Heaven, and casting out every carnal thought from the soul, dost you not with disembodied spirit and pure reason contemplate the things which are in Heaven? Oh! what a marvel! what love of God to man! He who sits on high with the Father is at that hour held in the hands of all and gives Himself to those who are willing to embrace and grasp Him. And this all do through the eyes of faith! Do these things seem to you fit to be despised, or such as to make it possible for

anyone to be uplifted against them?

Would you also learn from another miracle the exceeding sanctity of this office? Picture Elijah and the vast multitude standing around him, and the sacrifice laid upon the altar of stones, and all the rest of the people hushed into a deep silence while the prophet alone offers up prayer: then the sudden rush of fire from Heaven upon the sacrifice: —these are marvelous things, charged with terror. Now then pass from this scene to the rites which are celebrated in the present day; they are not only marvelous to behold, but transcendent in terror. There stands the priest, not bringing down fire from Heaven, but the Holy Spirit: and he makes prolonged supplication, not that some flame sent down from on high may consume the offerings, but that grace descending on the sacrifice may thereby enlighten the souls of all and render them more refulgent than silver purified by fire. Who can despise this most awful mystery, unless he is stark mad and senseless? Or do you not know that no human soul could have endured that fire in the sacrifice, but all would have been utterly consumed, had not the assistance of God's grace been great.

5. For if anyone will consider how great a thing it is for one, being a man, and compassed with flesh and blood, to be enabled to draw nigh to that blessed and pure nature, he will then clearly see what great honor the grace of the Spirit has vouchsafed to priests; since by their agency these rites are celebrated, and others nowise inferior to these both in respect of our dignity and our salvation. For they who inhabit the earth and make their abode there are entrusted with the administration of things which are in Heaven and have received an authority which God has not given to angels or archangels. For it

has not been said to them, "Whatsoever ye shall bind on earth shall be bound in Heaven, and whatsoever ye shall loose on earth shall be loosed in Heaven." They who rule on earth have indeed authority to bind, but only the body: whereas this binding lays hold of the soul and penetrates the heavens; and what priests do here below God ratifies above, and the Master confirms the sentence of his servants. For indeed what is it but all manner of heavenly authority which He has given them when He says, "Whose sins ye remit they are remitted, and whose sins ye retain they are retained?" What authority could be greater than this? "The Father hath committed all judgment to the Son?" But I see it all put into the hands of these men by the Son. For they have been conducted to this dignity as if they were already translated to Heaven, and had transcended human nature, and were released from the passions to which we are liable. Moreover, if a king should bestow this honor upon any of his subjects, authorizing him to cast into prison whom he pleased and to release them again, he becomes an object of envy and respect to all men; but he who has received from God an authority as much greater as heaven is more precious than earth, and souls more precious than bodies, seems to some to have received so small an honor that they are actually able to imagine that one of those who have been entrusted with these things will despise the gift. Away with such madness! For transparent madness it is to despise so great a dignity, without which it is not possible to obtain either our own salvation, or the good things which have been promised to us. For if no one can enter into the kingdom of Heaven except he be regenerate through water and the Spirit, and he who does not eat the flesh of the Lord and drink His blood is excluded from eternal life, and if all these things are accomplished only by means of those holy hands, I mean the hands of the priest, how will anyone, without these, be able to escape the fire of hell, or to win those crowns which are reserved for the victorious?

6. These verily are they who are entrusted with the pangs of spiritual travail and the birth which comes through baptism: by their means we put on Christ, and are buried with the Son of God, and become members of that blessed Head. Wherefore they might not only be more justly feared by us than rulers and kings, but also be more honored than parents; since these begat us of blood and the will of the flesh, but the others are the authors of our birth from God, even that blessed regeneration which is the true freedom and the sonship according to grace. The Jewish priests had authority to release the body from leprosy, or, rather, not to release it but only to examine those who were already released, and you know how much the office of priest was contended for at that time. But our priests have received authority to deal, not with bodily leprosy, but spiritual uncleanness—not to pronounce it removed after examination, but actually and absolutely to take it away. Wherefore they who despise these priests would be far more accursed than Dathan and his company and deserve more severe punishment. For the latter, although they laid claim to the dignity which did not belong to them, nevertheless had an excellent opinion concerning it, and this they evinced by the great eagerness with which they pursued it; but these men, when the office has been better regulated, and has received so great a development, have displayed an audacity which exceeds that of the others, although manifested in a contrary way. For there is not an equal

amount of contempt involved in aiming at an honor which does not pertain to one, and in despising such great advantages, but the latter exceeds the former as much as scorn differs from admiration. What soul then is so sordid as to despise such great advantages? None whatever, I should say, unless it were one subject to some demoniacal impulse. For I return once more to the point from which I started: not in the way of chastising only, but also in the way of benefiting, God has bestowed a power on priests greater than that of our natural parents. The two indeed differ as much as the present and the future life. For our natural parents generate us unto this life only, but the others unto that which is to come. And the former would not be able to avert death from their offspring, or to repel the assaults of disease; but these others have often saved a sick soul, or one which was on the point of perishing, procuring for some a milder chastisement, and preventing others from falling altogether, not only by instruction and admonition, but also by the assistance wrought through prayers. For not only at the time of regeneration, but afterwards also, they have authority to forgive sins. "Is any sick among you?" it is said, "let him call for the elders of the Church and let them pray over him, anointing him with oil in the name of the Lord. And the prayer of faith shall save the sick, and the Lord will raise him up: and if he has committed sins, they shall be forgiven him." Again: our natural parents, should their children come into conflict with any men of high rank and great power in the world, are unable to profit them: but priests have reconciled, not rulers and kings, but God Himself when His wrath has often been provoked against them.

Well! after this will anyone venture to condemn

me for arrogance? For my part, after what has been said, I imagine such religious fear will possess the souls of the hearers that they will no longer condemn those who avoid the office for arrogance and temerity, but rather those who voluntarily come forward and are eager to obtain this dignity for themselves. For if they who have been entrusted with the command of cities, should they chance to be wanting in discretion and vigilance, have sometimes destroyed the cities and ruined themselves in addition, how much power think you both in himself and from above must he need, to avoid sinning, whose business it is to beautify the Bride of Christ?

 7. No man loved Christ more than Paul: no man exhibited greater zeal, no man was counted worthy of more grace: nevertheless, after all these great advantages, he still has fears and trembling concerning this government and those who were governed by him. "I fear," he says, "lest by any means, as the serpent beguiled Eve through his subtlety, so your minds should be corrupted from the simplicity which is in Christ." And again, "I was with you in fear and in much trembling;" and this was a man who had been caught up to the third Heaven, and made partaker of the unspeakable mysteries of God, and had endured as many deaths as he had lived days after he became a believer—a man, moreover, who would not use the authority given him from Christ lest any of his converts should be offended. If, then, he who went beyond the ordinances of God, and nowhere sought his own advantage, but that of those whom he governed, was always so full of fear when he considered the greatness of his government, what shall our condition be who in many ways seek our own, who not only fail to go beyond the commandments of Christ, but for the most

part transgress them? "Who is weak," he says, "and I am not weak? who is offended, and I burn not?" Such an one ought the priest to be, or, rather, not such only: for these are small things, and as nothing compared with what I am about to say. And what is this? "I could wish," he says, "that myself were accursed from Christ for my brethren, my kinsmen according to the flesh." If anyone can utter such a speech, if anyone has the soul which attains to such a prayer, he might justly be blamed if he took to flight: but if anyone should lack such excellence as much as I do, he would deserve to be hated, not if he avoided the office, but if he accepted it. For if an election to a military dignity was the business in hand, and they who had the right of conferring the honor were to drag forward a brazier, or a shoemaker, or some such artisan, and entrust the army to his hands, I should not praise the wretched man if he did not take to flight, and do all in his power to avoid plunging into such manifest trouble. If, indeed, it be sufficient to bear the name of pastor, and to take the work in hand hap-hazard, and there be no danger in this, then let whoso pleases accuse me of vainglory; but if it behooves one who undertakes this care to have much understanding, and, before understanding, great grace from God, and uprightness of conduct, and purity of life and superhuman virtue, do not deprive me of forgiveness if I am unwilling to perish in vain without a cause.

Moreover, if anyone in charge of a full-sized merchant ship, full of rowers, and laden with a costly freight, were to station me at the helm and bid me cross the Ægean or the Tyrrhene sea, I should recoil from the proposal at once: and if anyone asked me why? I should say, "Lest I should sink the ship." Well, where the loss concerns material wealth, and the danger extends only to bodily death, no one will blame those who exercise great prudence; but where the shipwrecked are destined to fall, not into the ocean, but into the abyss of fire, and the death which awaits them is not that which severs the soul from the body, but one which together with this dismisses it to eternal punishment, shall I incur your wrath and hate because I did not plunge headlong into so great an evil?

8. Do not thus, I pray and beseech you. I know my own soul, how feeble and puny it is: I know the magnitude of this ministry, and the great difficulty of the work; for more stormy billows vex the soul of the priest than the gales which disturb the sea.

9. And first of all is that most terrible rock of vainglory, more dangerous than that of the Sirens, of which the fable-mongers tell such marvelous tales: for many were able to sail past that and escape unscathed; but this is to me so dangerous that even now, when no necessity of any kind impels me into that abyss, I am unable to keep clear of the snare: but if any one were to commit this charge to me, it would be all the same as if he tied my hands behind my back, and delivered me to the wild beasts dwelling on that rock to rend me in pieces day by day. Do you ask what those wild beasts are? They are wrath, despondency, envy, strife, slanders, accusations, falsehood, hypocrisy, intrigues, anger against those who have done no harm, pleasure at the indecorous acts of fellow ministers, sorrow at their prosperity, love of praise, desire of honor (which indeed most of all drives the human soul headlong to perdition), doctrines devised to please, servile flatteries, ignoble fawning, contempt of the poor, paying court to the rich, senseless and mischievous honors, favors attended with danger both to those who offer and those who accept them, sordid fear suited only

to the basest of slaves, the abolition of plain speaking, a great affectation of humility, but banishment of truth, the suppression of convictions and reproofs, or rather the excessive use of them against the poor, while against those who are invested with power no one dare open his lips.

For all these wild beasts, and more than these, are bred upon that rock of which I have spoken, and those whom they have once captured are inevitably dragged down into such a depth of servitude that even to please women they often do many things which it is well not to mention. The divine law indeed has excluded women from the ministry, but they endeavor to thrust themselves into it; and since they can effect nothing of themselves, they do all through the agency of others; and they have become invested with so much power that they can appoint or eject priests at their will: things in fact are turned upside down, and the proverbial saying may be seen realized—"The ruled lead the rulers:" and would that it were men who do this instead of women, who have not received a commission to teach. Why do I say teach? for the blessed Paul did not suffer them even to speak in the Church. But I have heard someone say that they have obtained such a large privilege of free speech, as even to rebuke the prelates of the Churches, and censure them more severely than masters do their own domestics.

10. And let not anyone suppose that I subject all to the aforesaid charges: for there are some, yea many, who are superior to these entanglements, and exceed in number those who have been caught by them. Nor would I indeed make the priesthood responsible for these evils: far be such madness from me. For men of understanding do not say that the sword is to blame for murder, nor wine

for drunkenness, nor strength for outrage, nor courage for foolhardiness, but they lay the blame on those who make an improper use of the gifts which have been bestowed upon them by God and punish them accordingly. Certainly, at least, the priesthood may justly accuse us if we do not rightly handle it. For it is not itself a cause of the evils already mentioned, but we, who as far as lies in our power have defiled it with so many pollutions, by entrusting it to commonplace men who readily accept what is offered them, without having first acquired a knowledge of their own souls, or considered the gravity of the office, and when they have entered on the work, being blinded by inexperience, overwhelm with innumerable evils the people who have been committed to their care. This is the very thing, which was very nearly happening in my case, had not God speedily delivered me from those dangers, mercifully sparing his Church and my own soul. For, tell me, whence do you think such great troubles are generated in the Churches? I, for my part, believe the only source of them to be the inconsiderate and random way in which prelates are chosen and appointed. For the head ought to be the strongest part, that it may be able to regulate and control the evil exhalations which arise from the rest of the body below; but when it happens to be weak in itself, and unable to repel those pestiferous attacks, it becomes feebler itself than it really is, and ruins the rest of the body as well. And to prevent this now coming to pass, God kept me in the position of the feet, which was the rank originally assigned to me. For there are very many other qualities, Basil, besides those already mentioned, which the priest ought to have, but which I do not possess; and, above all, this one:—his soul ought to be thoroughly purged from any lust after the office: for if he happens to have a natural inclination for this dignity, as soon as he attains it a stronger flame is kindled, and the man being taken completely captive will endure innumerable evils in order to keep a secure hold upon it, even to the extent of using flattery, or submitting to something base and ignoble, or expending large sums of money. For I will not now speak of the murders with which some have filled the Churches,105 or the desolation which they have brought upon cities in contending for the dignity, lest some persons should think what I say incredible. But I am of opinion one ought to exercise so much caution in the matter, as to shun the burden of the office,106 and when one has entered upon it, not to wait for the judgment of others should any fault be committed which warrants deposition, but to anticipate it by ejecting oneself from the dignity; for thus one might probably win mercy for himself from God: but to cling to it in defiance of propriety is to deprive oneself of all forgiveness, or rather to kindle the wrath of God, by adding a second error more offensive than the first.

11. But no one will always endure the strain; for fearful, truly fearful is the eager desire after this honor. And in saying this I am not in opposition to the blessed Paul, but in complete harmony with his words. For what says he? "If any man desires the office of a bishop, he desires a good work." Now I have not said that it is a terrible thing to desire the work, but only the authority and power. And this desire I think one ought to expel from the soul with all possible earnestness, not permitting it at the outset to be possessed by such a feeling, so that one may be able to do everything with freedom. For he who does not desire to be exhibited in possession of this authority, does not fear to be deposed from it, and not

fearing this will be able to do everything with the freedom which becomes Christian men: whereas they who fear and tremble lest they should be deposed undergo a bitter servitude, filled with all kinds of evils, and are often compelled to offend against both God and man. Now the soul ought not to be affected in this way; but as in warfare we see those soldiers who are noble-spirited fight willingly and fall bravely, so they who have attained to this stewardship should be contented to be consecrated to the dignity or removed from it, as becomes Christian men, knowing that deposition of this kind brings its reward no less than the discharge of the office. For when anyone suffers anything of this kind, in order to avoid submitting to something which is unbecoming or unworthy of this dignity, he procures punishment for those who wrongfully depose him, and a greater reward for himself. "Blessed," says our Lord, "are ye when men shall revile you and persecute you and shall say all manner of evil against you falsely for my sake; rejoice and be exceeding glad, for great is your reward in Heaven." And this, indeed, is the case when any one is expelled by those of his own rank either on account of envy, with a view to the favor of others, or through hatred, or from any other wrong motive: but when it is the lot of anyone to experience this treatment at the hand of opponents, I do not think a word is needed to prove what great gain they confer upon him by their wickedness.

It behooves us, then, to be on the watch on all sides, and to make a careful search lest any spark of this desire should be secretly smoldering somewhere. For it is much to be wished that those who are originally free from this passion, should also be able to avoid it when they have lighted upon this office. But if anyone, before he obtains the honor, cherishes in himself this terrible and savage monster, it is impossible to say into what a furnace he will fling himself after he has attained it. Now I possessed this desire in a high degree (and do not suppose that I would ever tell you what was untrue in self-disparagement): and this, combined with other reasons, alarmed me not a little, and induced me to take flight. For just as lovers of the human person, as long as they are permitted to be near the objects of their affection, suffer more severe torment from their passion, but when they remove as far as possible from these objects of desire, they drive away the frenzy: even so when those who desire this dignity are near it, the evil becomes intolerable: but when they cease to hope for it, the desire is extinguished together with the expectation.

12. This single motive then is no slight one: and even taken by itself it would have sufficed to deter me from this dignity: but, as it is, another must be added not less than the former. And what is this? A priest ought to be sober minded, and penetrating in discernment, and possessed of innumerable eyes in every direction, as one who lives not for himself alone but for so great a multitude. But that I am sluggish and slack, and scarcely able to bring about my own salvation, even you yourself would admit, who out of love to me art especially eager to conceal my faults. Talk not to me in this connection of fasting, and watching, or sleeping on the ground, and other hard discipline of the body: for you know how defective I am in these matters: and even if they had been carefully practiced by me they could not with my present sluggishness have been of any service to me with a view to this post of authority. Such things might be of great service to a man who was shut up in a cell, and caring

only for his own concerns: but when a man is divided among so great a multitude, and enters separately into the private cares of those who are under his direction, what appreciable help can be given to their improvement unless he possesses a robust and exceedingly vigorous character?

13. And do not be surprised if, in connection with such endurance, I seek another test of fortitude in the soul. For to be indifferent to food and drink and a soft bed, we see is to many no hard task, especially at least to such as are of a rough habit of life and have been brought up in this way from early youth, and to many others also; bodily discipline and custom softening the severity of these laborious practices: but insult, and abuse, and coarse language, and gibes from inferiors, whether wantonly or justly uttered, and rebukes vainly and idly spoken both by rulers and the ruled—this is what few can bear, in fact only one or two here and there; and one may see men, who are strong in the former exercises, so completely upset by these things, as to become more furious than the most savage beasts. Now such men especially we should exclude from the precincts of the priesthood. For if a prelate did not loathe food, or go barefoot, no harm would be done to the common interests of the Church; but a furious temper causes great disasters both to him who possesses it, and to his neighbors. And there is no divine threat against those who fail to do the things referred to, but hell and hellfire are threatened against those who are angry without a cause. As then the lover of vainglory, when he takes upon him the government of numbers, supplies additional fuel to the fire, so he who by himself, or in the company of a few, is unable to control his anger, but readily carried away by it, should he be entrusted with the direction of a whole multitude, like some wild beast

goaded on all sides by countless tormentors, would never be able to live in tranquility himself, and would cause incalculable mischief to those who have been committed to his charge.

14. For nothing clouds the purity of the reason, and the perspicuity of the mental vision so much as undisciplined wrath, rushing along with violent impetuosity. "For wrath," says one, "destroys even the prudent." For the eye of the soul being darkened as in some nocturnal battle is not able to distinguish friends from foes, nor the honorable from the unworthy, but handles them all in turn in the same way; even if some harm must be suffered, readily enduring everything, in order to satisfy the pleasure of the soul. For the fire of wrath is a kind of pleasure, and tyrannizes over the soul more harshly than pleasure, completely upsetting its healthy organization. For it easily impels men to arrogance, and unseasonable enmities, and unreasonable hatred, and it continually makes them ready to commit wanton and vain offences; and forces them to say and do many other things of that kind, the soul being swept along by the rush of passion, and having nothing on which to fasten its strength and resist so great an impulse.

Basil: I will not endure this irony of yours any longer: for who knows not how far removed you are from this infirmity?

Chrysostom: Why then, my good friend, do you wish to bring me near the pyre, and to provoke the wild beast when he is tranquil? Are you not aware that I have achieved this condition, not by any innate virtue, but by my love of retirement? and that when one who is so constituted remains contented by himself, or only associates with one or two friends, he is able to escape the fire which arises from this passion, but not if he has plunged into the abyss of all these cares? for then he drags not only himself but many others with him to the brink of destruction, and renders them more indifferent to all consideration for mildness. For the mass of people under government are generally inclined to regard the manners of those who govern as a kind of model type, and to assimilate themselves to them. How then could anyone put a stop to their fury when he is swelling himself with rage? And who amongst the multitude would straightway desire to become moderate when he sees the ruler irritable? For it is quite impossible for the defects of priests to be concealed, but even trifling ones speedily become manifest. So an athlete, as long as he remains at home, and contends with no one, can dissemble his weakness even if it be very great, but when he strips for the contest he is easily detected. And thus, for some who live this private and inactive life, their isolation serves as a veil to hide their defects; but when they have been brought into public, they are compelled to divest themselves of this mantle of seclusion, and to lay bare their souls to all through their visible movements. As therefore their right deeds profit many, by provoking them to equal zeal, so their shortcomings make men more indifferent to the practice of virtue and encourage them to indolence in their endeavors after what is excellent. Wherefore his soul ought to gleam with beauty on every side, that it may be able to gladden and to enlighten the souls of those who behold it. For the faults of ordinary men, being committed as it were in the dark, ruin only those who practice them: but the errors of a man in a conspicuous position, and known to many, inflicts a common injury upon all, rendering those who have fallen more supine in their efforts for good, and driving to desperation those who wish to take heed to themselves. And apart from these things, the faults of insignificant men, even if they are exposed, inflict no injury worth speaking of upon any one: but they who occupy the highest seat of honor are in the first place plainly visible to all, and if they err in the smallest matters these trifles seem great to others: for all men measure the sin, not by the magnitude of the offence, but by the rank of the offender. Thus the priest ought to be protected on all sides by a kind of adamantine armor, by intense earnestness, and perpetual watchfulness concerning his manner of life, lest someone discovering an exposed and neglected spot should inflict a deadly wound: for all who surround him are ready to smite and overthrow him: not enemies only and adversaries, but many even of those who profess friendship.

The souls therefore of men elected to the priesthood ought to be endued with such power as the grace of God bestowed on the bodies of those saints who were cast into the Babylonian furnace. Faggot and pitch and tow are not the fuel of this fire, but things far more dreadful: for it is no material fire to which they are subjected, but the all-devouring flame of envy encompasses them, rising up on every side, and assailing them, and putting their life to a more searching test than the fire then was to the bodies of those young men. When then it finds a little trace of stubble, it speedily fastens upon it; and this unsound part it entirely consumes, but all the rest of the fabric, even if it be brighter than the sunbeams, is scorched and blackened by the smoke. For as long as the life of the priest is well regulated in every direction, it is invulnerable to plots; but if he happens to overlook some trifle, as is natural in a human being, traversing the treacherous ocean of this life, none of his other good deeds are of any avail in enabling him to escape the mouths of his accusers; but that little blunder overshadows all the rest. And all men are ready to pass judgment on the priest as if he was not a being clothed with flesh, or one who inherited a human nature, but like an angel, and emancipated from every species of infirmity. And just as all men fear and flatter a tyrant as long as he is strong, because they cannot put him down, but when they see his affairs going adversely, those who were his friends a short time before abandon their hypocritical respect, and suddenly become his enemies and antagonists, and having discovered all his weak points, make an attack upon him, and depose him from the government; so is it also in the case of priests. Those who honored him and paid court to him a short time before, while he was strong, as soon as they have found some little handle eagerly prepare to depose him, not as a tyrant only, but something far more dreadful than that. And as the tyrant fears his bodyguards, so also does the priest dread most of all his neighbors and fellow ministers. For no others covet his dignity so much or know his affairs so well as these; and if anything occurs, being near at hand, they perceive it before others, and even if they slander him, can easily command belief, and, by magnifying trifles, take their victim captive. For the apostolic saying is reversed, "whether one member suffer, all the members suffer with it; or one member be honored, all the members rejoice with it;" unless indeed a man should be able by his great discretion to stand his ground against everything.

Are you then for sending me forth into so great a

warfare? and did you think that my soul would be equal to a contest so various in character and shape? Whence did you learn this, and from whom? If God certified this to you, show me the oracle, and I obey; but if you cannot, and form your judgment from human opinion only, please to set yourself free from this delusion. For in what concerns my own affairs it is fairer to trust me than others; inasmuch as "no man knows the things of a man, save the spirit of man which is in him." That I should have made myself and my electors ridiculous, had I accepted this office, and should with great loss have returned to this condition of life in which I now am, I trust I have now convinced you by these remarks, if not before. For not malice only, but something much stronger—the lust after this dignity—is wont to arm many against one who possesses it. And just as avaricious children are oppressed by the old age of their parents, so some of these, when they see the priestly office held by any one for a protracted time—since it would be wickedness to destroy him—hasten to depose him from it, being all desirous to take his place, and each expecting that the dignity will be transferred to himself.

15. Would you like me to show you yet another phase of this strife, charged with innumerable dangers? Come, then, and take a peep at the public festivals when it is generally the custom for elections to be made to ecclesiastical dignities, and you will then see the priest assailed with accusations as numerous as the people whom he rules. For all who have the privilege of conferring the honor are then split into many parties; and one can never find the council of elders of one mind with each other, or about the man who has won the prelacy; but each stands apart from the others, one preferring this man,

another that. Now the reason is that they do not all look to one thing, which ought to be the only object kept in view, the excellence of the character; but other qualifications are alleged as recommending to this honor; for instance, of one it is said, "let him be elected because he belongs to an illustrious family," of another "because he is possessed of great wealth, and would not need to be supported out of the revenues of the Church," of a third "because he has come over from the camp of the adversary;" one is eager to give the preference to a man who is on terms of intimacy with himself, another to the man who is related to him by birth, a third to the flatterer, but no one will look to the man who is really qualified, or make some test of his character. Now I am so far from thinking these things trustworthy criteria of a man's fitness for the priesthood, that even if anyone manifested great piety, which is no small help in the discharge of that office, I should not venture to approve him on that account alone, unless he happened to combine good abilities with his piety. For I know many men who have exercised perpetual restraint upon themselves, and consumed themselves with fasting, who, as long as they were suffered to be alone, and attend to their own concerns, have been acceptable to God, and day by day have made no small addition to this kind of learning; but as soon as they entered public life, and were compelled to correct the ignorance of the multitude, have, some of them, proved from the outset incompetent for so great a task, and others when forced to persevere in it, have abandoned their former strict way of living, and thus inflicted great injury on themselves without profiting others at all. And if anyone spent his whole time in the lowest rank of the ministry, and reached extreme old age, I would not, merely out of reverence for his years, promote him to the higher dignity; for what if, after arriving at that time of life, he should still remain unfit for the office? And I say this now, not as wishing to dishonor the grey head, nor as laying down a law absolutely to exclude from this authority those who come from the monastic circle (for there are instances of many who issued from that body, having shone conspicuously in this dignity); but the point which I am anxious to prove is, that if neither piety of itself, nor advanced age, would suffice to show that a man who had obtained the priesthood really deserved it, the reasons formerly alleged would scarcely effect this. There are also men who bring forward other pretexts yet more absurd; for some are enrolled in the ranks of the clergy, that they may not range themselves among opponents, and others on account of their evil disposition, lest they should do great mischief if they are overlooked. Could anything be more contrary to right rule than this? that bad men, laden with iniquity, should be courted on account of those things for which they ought to be punished, and ascend to the priestly dignity on account of things for which they ought to be debarred from the very threshold of the Church. Tell me, then, shall we seek any further the cause of God's wrath, when we expose things so holy and awful to be defiled by men who are either wicked or worthless? for when some men are entrusted with the administration of things which are not at all suitable to them, and others of things which exceed their natural power, they make the condition of the Church like that of Euripus.

Now formerly I used to deride secular rulers, because in the distribution of their honors they are not guided by considerations of moral excellence, but of wealth, and seniority, and human distinction; but when I heard that this kind of folly had forced its way into our affairs also, I no longer regarded their conduct as so atrocious. For what wonder is it that worldly men, who love the praise of the multitude, and do everything for the sake of gain, should commit these sins, when those who affect at least to be free from all these influences are in no wise better disposed than they, but although engaged in a contest for heavenly things, act as if the question submitted for decision was one which concerned acres of land, or something else of that kind? for they take commonplace men off-hand, and set them to preside over those things, for the sake of which the only begotten Son of God did not refuse to empty Himself of His glory and become man, and take the form of a servant, and be spat upon, and buffeted, and die a death of reproach in the flesh. Nor do they stop even here but add to these offences others still more monstrous; for not only do they elect unworthy men, but actually expel those who are well qualified. As if it were necessary to ruin the safety of the Church on both sides, or as if the former provocation were not sufficient to kindle the wrath of God, they have contrived yet another not less pernicious. For I consider it as atrocious to expel the useful men as to force in the useless. And this in fact takes place, so that the flock of Christ is unable to find consolation in any direction or draw its breath freely. Now do not such deeds deserve to be punished by ten thousand thunderbolts, and a hell-fire hotter than that with which we are threatened [in Holy Scripture]? Yet these monstrous evils are borne with by Him who wills not the death of a sinner, that he may be converted and live. And how can one sufficiently marvel at His lovingkindness, and be amazed at His mercy? They who belong to Christ destroy the property of Christ more than enemies and adversaries, yet the good Lord still deals gently with them, and calls them to repentance. Glory be to You, O Lord! Glory to You! How vast is the depth of Thy lovingkindness! how great the riches of Thy forbearance! Men who on account of Thy name have risen from insignificance and obscurity to positions of honor and distinction, use the honor they enjoy against Him who has bestowed it, do deeds of outrageous audacity, and insult holy things, rejecting and expelling men of zeal in order that the wicked may ruin everything at their pleasure in much security, and with the utmost fearlessness. And if you would know the causes of this dreadful evil, you will find that they are similar to those which were mentioned before; for they have one root and mother, so to say—namely, envy; but this is manifested in several different forms. For one we are told is to be struck out of the list of candidates, because he is young; another because he does not know how to flatter; a third because he has offended such and such a person; a fourth lest such and such a man should be pained at seeing one whom he has presented rejected, and this man elected; a fifth because he is kind and gentle; a sixth because he is formidable to the sinful; a seventh for some other like reason; for they are at no loss to find as many pretexts as they want, and can even make the abundance of a man's wealth an objection when they have no other. Indeed, they would be capable of discovering other reasons, as many as they wish, why a man ought not to be brought suddenly to this honor, but gently and gradually. And here I should like to ask the question, "What, then, is the prelate to do, who has to contend with such blasts? How shall he hold his ground against such billows? How shall he repel all these assaults?"

For if he manages the business upon upright principles, all those who are enemies and adversaries both to him and to the candidates do everything with a view to contention, provoking daily strife, and heaping infinite scorn upon the candidates, until they have got them struck off the list, or have introduced their own favorites. In fact, it is just as if some pilot had pirates sailing with him in his ship, perpetually plotting every hour against him, and the sailors, and marines. And if he should prefer favor with such men to his own salvation, accepting unworthy candidates, he will have God for his enemy in their stead; and what could be more dreadful than that? And yet his relations with them will be more embarrassing than formerly, as they will all combine with each other, and thereby become more powerful than before. For as when fierce winds coming from opposite directions clash with one another, the ocean, hitherto calm, becomes suddenly furious and raises its crested waves, destroying those who are sailing over it, so also when the Church has admitted corrupt men, its once tranquil surface is covered with rough surf and strewn with shipwrecks.

16. Consider, then, what kind of man he ought to be who is to hold out against such a tempest, and to manage skillfully such great hindrances to the common welfare; for he ought to be dignified yet free from arrogance, formidable yet kind, apt to command yet sociable, impartial yet courteous, humble yet not servile, strong yet gentle, in order that he may contend successfully against all these difficulties. And he ought to bring forward with great authority the man who is properly qualified for the office, even if all should oppose him, and with the same authority to reject the man who is

not so qualified, even if all should conspire in his favor, and to keep one aim only in view, the building up of the Church, in nothing actuated either by enmity or favor. Well, do you now think that I acted reasonably in declining the ministry of this office? But I have not even yet gone through all my reasons with you; for I have some others still to mention. And do not grow impatient of listening to a friendly and sincere man, who wishes to clear himself from your accusations; for these statements are not only serviceable for the defense which you have to make on my behalf, but they will also prove of no small help for the due administration of the office. For it is necessary for one who is going to enter upon this path of life to investigate all matters thoroughly well, before he sets his hand to the ministry. Do you ask why? Because one who knows all things clearly will have this advantage, if no other, that he will not feel strange when these things befall him. Would you like me then to approach the question of superintending widows, first of all, or of the care of virgins, or the difficulty of the judicial function. For in each of these cases there is a different kind of anxiety, and the fear is greater than the anxiety.

Now in the first place, to start from that subject which seems to be simpler than the others, the charge of widows appears to cause anxiety to those who take care of them only so far as the expenditure of money is concerned; but the case is otherwise, and here also a careful scrutiny is needed, when they have to be enrolled, for infinite mischief has been caused by putting them on the list without due discrimination. For they have ruined households, and severed marriages, and have often been detected in thieving and pilfering and unseemly deeds of that kind. Now that such women should be supported out of the Church's revenues provokes punishment from God, and extreme condemnation among men, and abates the zeal of those who wish to do good. For whom would ever choose to expend the wealth which he was commanded to give to Christ upon those who defame the name of Christ? For these reasons a strict and accurate scrutiny ought to be made so as to prevent the supply of the indigent being wasted, not only by the women already mentioned, but also by those who are able to provide for themselves. And this scrutiny is succeeded by no small anxiety of another kind, to ensure an abundant and unfailing stream of supply as from a fountain; for compulsory poverty is an insatiable kind of evil, querulous and ungrateful. And great discretion and great zeal is required so as to stop the mouths of complainers, depriving them of every excuse. Now most men, when they see any one superior to the love of money, forthwith represent him as well qualified for this stewardship. But I do not think that this greatness of soul is ever sufficient of itself, although it ought to be possessed prior to all other qualities; for without this a man would be a destroyer rather than a protector, a wolf instead of a shepherd; nevertheless, combined with this, the possession of another quality also should be demanded. And this quality is forbearance, the cause of all good things in men, impelling as it were and conducting the soul into a serene haven. For widows are a class who, both on account of their poverty, their age and natural disposition, indulge in unlimited freedom of speech (so I had best call it); and they make an unseasonable clamor and idle complaints and lamentations about matters for which they ought to be grateful, and bring accusations concerning things which they ought contentedly to accept. Now the superintendent should endure all these things in a generous spirit, and not be provoked either by their unreasonable annoyance or their unreasonable complaints. For this class of persons deserve to be pitied for their misfortunes, not to be insulted; and to trample upon their calamities and add the pain of insult to that which poverty brings, would be an act of extreme brutality. On this account one of the wisest of men, having regard to the avarice and pride of human nature, and considering the nature of poverty and its terrible power to depress even the noblest character, and induce it often to act in these same respects without shame, in order that a man should not be irritated when accused, nor be provoked by continual importunity to become an enemy where he ought to bring aid, he instructs him to be affable and accessible to the suppliant, saying, "Incline thine ear to a poor man and give him a friendly answer with meekness." And passing by the case of one who succeeds in exasperating (for what can one say to him who is overcome?), he addresses the man who is able to bear the other's infirmity, exhorting him before he bestows his gift to correct the suppliant by the gentleness of his countenance and the mildness of his words. But if anyone, although he does not take the property (of these widows), nevertheless loads them with innumerable reproaches, and insults them, and is exasperated against them, he not only fails through his gift to alleviate the despondency produced by poverty but aggravates the distress by his abuse. For although they may be compelled to act very shamelessly through the necessity of hunger, they are nevertheless distressed at this compulsion. When then, owing to the dread of famine, they are constrained to beg, and owing to their begging are constrained to put off shame, and then again on account of their shamelessness are insulted, the power of despondency becoming of a complex kind, and accompanied by much gloom, settles down upon the soul. And one who has the charge of these persons ought to be so long-suffering, as not only not to increase their despondency by his fits of anger, but also to remove the greater part of it by his exhortation. For as the man who has been insulted, although he is in the enjoyment of great abundance, does not feel the advantage of his wealth, on account of the blow which he has received from the insult; so on the other hand, the man who has been addressed with kindly words, and for whom the gift has been accompanied with encouragement, exults and rejoices all the more, and the thing given becomes doubled in value through the manner in which it is offered. And this I say not of myself but borrow from him whose precept I quoted just now: "My son, blemish not thy good deeds, neither use uncomfortable words when you give anything. Shall not the dew assuage the heat? So is a word better than a gift. Lo! is not a word better than a gift? but both are with a gracious man."

But the superintendent of these persons ought not only to be gentle and forbearing, but also skillful in the management of property; for if this qualification is wanting, the affairs of the poor are again involved in the same distress. One who was entrusted not long ago with this ministry, and got together a large hoard of money, neither consumed it himself, nor expended it with a few exceptions upon those who needed it, but kept the greater part of it buried in the earth until a season of distress occurred, when it was all surrendered into the hands of the enemy. Much forethought, therefore, is needed, that the resources of the Church should be neither over abundant, nor deficient, but that all the supplies which are provided should be quickly distributed among those who require them, and the treasures of the Church stored up in the hearts of those who are under her rule. Moreover, in the reception of strangers, and the care of the sick, consider how great an expenditure of money is needed, and how much exactness and discernment on the part of those who preside over these matters. For it is often necessary that this expenditure should be even larger than that of which I spoke just now, and that he who presides over it should combine prudence and wisdom with skill in the art of supply, so as to dispose the affluent to be emulous and ungrudging in their gifts, lest while providing for the relief of the sick, he should vex the souls of those who supply their wants. But earnestness and zeal need to be displayed here in a far higher degree; for the sick are difficult creatures to please, and prone to languor; and unless great accuracy and care are used, even a slight oversight is enough to do the patient great mischief.

17. But in the care of virgins, the fear is greater in proportion as the possession is more precious, and this flock is of a nobler character than the others. Already, indeed, even into the band of these holy ones, an infinite number of women have rushed full of innumerable bad qualities; and in this case our grief is greater than in the other; for there is just the same difference between a virgin and a widow going astray, as between a free-born damsel and her handmaid. With widows, indeed, it has become a common practice to trifle, and to rail at one another, to flatter or to be impudent, to appear everywhere in public, and to perambulate the marketplace. But the virgin has striven for nobler aims, and eagerly sought the highest kind of philosophy, and professes to exhibit upon

earth the life which angels lead, and while yet in the flesh proposes to do deeds which belong to the incorporeal powers. Moreover, she ought not to make numerous or unnecessary journeys, neither is it permissible for her to utter idle and random words; and as for abuse and flattery, she should not even know them by name. On this account she needs the most careful guardianship, and the greater assistance. For the enemy of holiness is always surprising and lying in wait for these persons, ready to devour any one of them if she should slip and fall; many men also there are who lay snares for them; and besides all these things there is the passionateness of their own human nature, so that, speaking generally, the virgin has to equip herself for a twofold war, one which attacks her from without, and the other which presses upon her from within. For these reasons he who has the superintendence of virgins suffers great alarm, and the danger and distress are yet greater, should any of the things which are contrary to his wishes occur, which God forbid. For if a daughter kept in seclusion is a cause of sleeplessness to her father, his anxiety about her depriving him of sleep, where the fear is so great lest she should be childless, or pass the flower of her age (unmarried), or be hated (by her husband), what will he suffer whose anxiety is not concerned with any of these things, but others far greater? For in this case, it is not a man who is rejected, but Christ Himself, nor is this barrenness the subject merely of reproach, but the evil ends in the destruction of the soul; "for every tree," it is said, "which bringeth not forth good fruit, is hewn down and cast into the fire." And for one who has been repudiated by the divine Bridegroom, it is not sufficient to receive a certificate of divorce and so to depart, but she has to pay the penalty of everlasting punishment. Moreover, a father according to the flesh has many things which make the custody of his daughter easy; for the mother, and nurse, and a multitude of handmaids share in helping the parent to keep the maiden safe. For neither is she permitted to be perpetually hurrying into the marketplace, nor when she does go there is she compelled to show herself to any of the passers-by, the evening darkness concealing one who does not wish to be seen no less than the walls of the house. And apart from these things, she is relieved from every cause which might otherwise compel her to meet the gaze of men; for no anxiety about the necessaries of life, no menaces of oppressors, nor anything of that kind reduces her to this unfortunate necessity, her father acting in her stead in all these matters; while she herself has only one anxiety, which is to avoid doing or saying anything unworthy the modest conduct which becomes her. But in the other case there are many things which make the custody of the virgin difficult, or rather impossible for the father; for he could not have her in his house with himself, as dwelling together in that way would be neither seemly nor safe. For even if they themselves should suffer no loss, but continue to preserve their innocence unsullied, they would have to give an account for the souls which they have offended, just as much as if they happened to sin with one another. And it being impossible for them to live together, it is not easy to understand the movements of the character, and to suppress the impulses which are ill regulated, or train and improve those which are better ordered and tuned. Nor is it an easy thing to interfere in her habits of walking out; for her poverty and want of a guardian does not permit him to become an exact investigator of the propriety of her conduct. For as she is compelled to manage all her affairs, she has many pretexts for going out, if at least she is not inclined to be self-controlled. Now he who commands her to stay always at home ought to cut off these pretexts, providing for her independence in the necessaries of life, and giving her some woman who will see to the management of these things. He must also keep her away from funeral obsequies, and nocturnal festivals; for that artful serpent knows only too well how to scatter his poison through the medium even of good deeds. And the maiden must be fenced on every side, and rarely go out of the house during the whole year, except when she is constrained by inexorable necessity. Now if any

58

one should say that none of these things is the proper work of a bishop to take in hand, let him be assured that the anxieties and the reasons concerning what takes place in every case have to be referred to him. And it is far more expedient that he should manage everything, and so be delivered from the complaints which he must otherwise undergo on account of the faults of others, than that he should abstain from the management, and then have to dread being called to account for things which other men have done. Moreover, he who does these things by himself, gets through them all with great ease; but he who is compelled to do it by converting every one's opinion does not get relief by being saved from working single-handed, equivalent to the trouble and turmoil which he experiences through those who oppose him and combat his decisions. However, I could not enumerate all the anxieties concerned with the care of virgins; for when they have to be entered on the list, they occasion no small trouble to him who is entrusted with this business.

Again, the judicial department of the bishop's office involves innumerable vexations, great consumption of time, and difficulties exceeding those experienced by men who sit to judge secular affairs; for it is a labor to discover exact justice, and when it is found, it is difficult to avoid destroying it. And not only loss of time and difficulty are incurred, but also no small danger. For ere now, some of the weaker brethren having plunged into business, because they have not obtained patronage have made shipwreck concerning the faith. For many of those who have suffered wrong, no less than those who have inflicted wrong, hate those who do not assist them, and they will not take into account either the intricacy of the matters in question, or the difficulty of the times, or the limits of sacerdotal authority, or anything of that kind; but they are merciless judges, recognizing only one kind of defense—release from the evils which oppress them. And he who is unable to furnish this, although he may allege innumerable excuses, will never escape their condemnation.

And talking of patronage, let me disclose another pretext for fault-finding. For if the bishop does not pay a round of visits every day, more even than the idle men about town, unspeakable offence ensues. For not only the sick, but also the whole, desire to be looked after, not that piety prompts them to this, but rather that in most cases they pretend claims to honor and distinction. And if he should ever happen to visit more constantly one of the richer and more powerful men, under the pressure of some necessity, with a view to the common benefit of the Church, he is immediately stigmatized with a character for fawning and flattery. But why do I speak of patronage and visiting? For merely from their mode of accosting persons, bishops have to endure such a load of reproaches as to be often oppressed and overwhelmed by despondency; in fact, they have also to undergo a scrutiny of the way in which they use their eyes. For the public rigorously criticize their simplest actions, taking note of the tone of their voice, the cast of their countenance, and the degree of their laughter. He laughed heartily to such a man, one will say, and accosted him with a beaming face, and a clear voice, whereas to me he addressed only a slight and passing remark. And in a large assembly, if he does not turn his eyes in every direction when he is conversing, the majority declare that his conduct is insulting.

Who, then, unless he is exceedingly strong, could cope with so many accusers, so as either to avoid being indited altogether, or, if he is indited, to escape? For he must either be without any accusers, or, if this is impossible, purge himself of the accusations which are brought against him; and if this again is not an easy matter, as some men delight in making vain and wanton charges, he must make a brave stand against the dejection produced by these complaints. He, indeed, who is justly accused, may easily tolerate the accuser, for there is no bitterer accuser than conscience; wherefore, if we are caught first by this most terrible adversary, we can readily endure the milder ones who are external to us. But he who has no evil thing upon his conscience, when he is subjected to an empty charge, is speedily excited to wrath, and easily sinks into dejection, unless he happens to have practiced beforehand how to put up with the follies of the multitude. For it is utterly impossible for one who is falsely accused without cause, and condemned, to avoid feeling some vexation and annoyance at such great injustice.

And how can one speak of the distress which bishops undergo, whenever it is necessary to cut some one off from the full communion of the Church? Would indeed that the evil went no further than distress! but in fact the mischief is not trifling. For there is a fear lest the man, if he has been punished beyond what he deserves, should experience that which was spoken of by the blessed Paul and "be swallowed up by overmuch sorrow." The nicest accuracy, therefore, is required in this matter also, lest what is intended to be profitable should become to him an occasion of greater damage. For whatever sins he may commit after such a method of treatment, the wrath caused by each of them must be shared by the physician who so unskillfully applied his knife to the wound. What severe punishment, then, must be expected by one who has not only to render an account of the offences which he himself has separately committed, but also incurs extreme danger on account of the sins committed by others? For if we shudder at undergoing judgment for our own misdeeds, believing that we shall not be able to escape the fire of the other world, what must one expect to suffer who has to answer for so many others? To prove the truth of this, listen to the blessed Paul, or rather not to him, but to Christ speaking in him, when he says: "Obey them that have the rule over you, and submit, for they watch for your souls as they that shall give account." Can the dread of this threat be slight? It is impossible to say: but these considerations are sufficient to convince even the most incredulous and obdurate that I did not make this escape under the influence of pride or vainglory, but merely out of fear for my own safety, and consideration of the gravity of the office.

Book IV.

Basil heard this, and after a little pause thus replied:

If you wert thyself ambitious of obtaining this office, thy fear would have been reasonable; for in being ambitious of undertaking it, a man confesses himself to be qualified for its administration, and if he fail therein, after it has been entrusted to him, he cannot take refuge in the plea of inexperience, for he has deprived himself of this excuse beforehand, by having hurriedly seized upon the ministry, and whoever willingly and deliberately enters upon it, can no longer say, "I have sinned in this matter against my will—and against my will I have ruined such and such a soul;" for He who will one day judge him, will say to him, "Since then you were conscious of such inexperience, and had not ability for undertaking this matter without incurring reproach, why wert you so eager and presumptuous as to take in hand what was so far beyond thy power? Who compelled you to do so? Did you shrink or fly, and did anyone drag you on by force?" But you will hear nothing like this, for you canst have nothing of this kind to condemn thyself for; and it is evident to all that you wert in no degree ambitious of this dignity, for the accomplishment of the matter was due to the action of others. Hence, circumstances which leave those who are ambitious of this office no chance of pardon when they err therein, afford you ample ground for excuse.

Chrysostom: At this I shook my head and smiled a little, admiring the simple-mindedness of the man, and thus addressed him: I could wish indeed that matters were as you sayest, most excellent of men, but not in order that I might be able to accept that office from which I lately fled. For if, indeed, no chastisement were to await me for undertaking the care of the flock of Christ without consideration and experience, yet to me it would be worse than all punishment, after being entrusted with so great a charge, to have seemed so base towards Him who entrusted me with it. For what reason, then, did I wish that you wert not mistaken in this opinion of thine? truly for the sake of those wretched and unhappy beings (for so must I call them, who have not found out how to discharge the duties of this office well, though you were to say ten thousand times over that they had been driven to undertake it, and that, therefore, their errors therein are sins of ignorance)—for the sake, I say, of such that they might succeed in escaping that unquenchable fire, and the outer darkness and the worm that dies not and the punishment of being cut asunder, and perishing together with the hypocrites.

But what am I to do for you? It is not as you sayest; no, by no means. And if you wilt, I will give you a proof of what I maintain, from the case of a kingdom, which is not of such account with God as the priesthood. Saul, that son of Kish, was not himself at all ambitious of becoming a king, but was going in quest of his asses, and came to ask the prophet about them. The prophet, however, proceeded to speak to him of the kingdom, but not even then did he run greedily after it, though he heard about it from a prophet, but drew back and deprecated it, saying, "Who am I, and what is my father's house."[129] What then? When he made a bad use of the honor which had been given him by God, were those words of his able to rescue him from the wrath of Him who had made him king? And was he able to say to Samuel, when rebuked by him: "Did I greedily run and rush after the kingdom and sovereign power? I wished to lead the undisturbed and peaceful life of ordinary men, but you didst drag me to this post of honor. Had I remained in my low estate I should easily have escaped all these stumbling blocks, for were I one of the obscure multitude, I should never have been sent forth on this expedition, nor would God have committed to my hands the war against the Amalekites, and if I had not had it committed to me, I should not have sinned this sin." But all such arguments are weak as excuses, and not only weak, but perilous, inasmuch as they rather kindle the wrath of God. For he who has been promoted to great honor by God, must not advance the greatness of his honor as an excuse for his errors, but should make God's special favor towards him the motive for further improvement; whereas he who thinks himself at liberty to sin because he has obtained some uncommon dignity, what does he but study to show that the lovingkindness of God is the cause of his personal transgression, which is always the argument of those who lead godless and careless lives. But we ought to be on no account thus minded, nor to fall away into the insane folly of such people but be ambitious at all times to make the most of such powers as we have, and to be reverent both in speech and thought.

    For (to leave the kingdom and to come to the priesthood, which is the more immediate subject of our discourse) neither was Eli ambitious of obtaining his high office, yet what advantage was this to him when he sinned therein? But why do I say obtain it? not even had he wished could he have avoided it, because he was under a legal necessity to accept it. For he was of the tribe of Levi and was bound to undertake that high office which descended to him from his forefathers, notwithstanding which even he paid no small penalty for the lawlessness of his sons. And the very first High Priest of the Jews, concerning whom God spoke so many words to Moses, when he was unable to withstand alone the frenzy of so great a multitude, was he not very nearly being destroyed, but for the intercession of his brother, which averted the wrath of God? And since we have mentioned Moses, it will be well to show the truth of what we are saying from what happened to him. For this same saintly Moses was so far from grasping at the leadership of the Jews as to deprecate the offer, and to decline it when God commanded him to take it, and so to provoke the wrath of Him who appointed him; and not only then, but afterwards when he entered upon his rule, he would gladly have died to have been set free from it: "Kill me," saith he, "if you are going to deal thus with me." But what then? when he sinned at the waters of strife, could these repeated refusals be pleaded in excuse for him? Could they prevail with God to grant him pardon? And wherefore was he deprived of the promised land? for no other reason, as we all know, than for this sin of his, for which that wondrous man was debarred from enjoying the same blessings which those over whom he ruled obtained; but after many labors and sufferings, after that unspeakable wandering, after so many battles fought and victories won, he died outside the land to reach which he had undergone so much toil and trial; and though he had weathered the storms of the deep, he failed to enjoy the blessings of the haven after all. From hence then you sees that not only they who grasp at this office are left without excuse for the sins they commit in the discharge thereof, but they too who come to it through the ambitious desire of others; for truly if those persons who have been chosen for this high office by God himself, though they have never so often refused it, have paid such heavy penalties, and if nothing has availed to deliver any of them from this danger, neither Aaron nor Eli, nor that holy man the Saint, the prophet, the wonder worker, the meek above all the men which were upon the face of the earth, who spoke with God, as a man speaks unto his friend, hardly shall we who fall so infinitely short of the excellence of that great man, be able to plead as a sufficient excuse the consciousness that we have never been ambitious of the dignity, more especially when many of the ordinations now-adays do not proceed from the grace of God, but are due to human ambition. God chose Judas, and counted him one of the sacred band, and committed to him, as to the rest, the dignity of the apostolic office; yea he gave him somewhat beyond the others, the stewardship of the money. But what of that? when he afterwards abused both these trusts, betraying Him whom he was commissioned to preach, and misapplying the money which he should have laid out well; did he escape punishment? nay for this very reason he even brought upon himself greater punishment, and very reasonably too. For we must not use the high honors given to us by God so as to offend Him, but so as to please Him better. But he who claims exemption from punishment where it is due, because he has been exalted to higher honor than others, acts very much like one of those unbelieving Jews, who after hearing Christ say, "If I had not come and spoken unto them, they had not had sin," "If I had not done among them the works which none other did, they had not had sin," should reproach the Savior and benefactor of mankind by replying, "Why, then, didst you come and speak? why didst you work miracles? was it that you might punish us the more?" But these are the words of madness and of utter senselessness. For the Great Physician came not to give you over, but to heal you—not to pass you by when you were sick, but to rid you entirely of disease. But you hast of thine own accord withdrawn thyself from his hands; receive therefore the sorer punishment. For as you would have been freed from thy former maladies if you had yielded to his treatment, so if, when you saw him coming to thine aid you fled from him, you will no longer be able to cleanse thyself of these infirmities, and as you art unable, you wilt both suffer punishment for them, and also because for thy part you made God's solicitude for thy good of none effect. Therefore, we who act like this are not subjected to the same torment after as before we received honor at God's hands, but far severer torment after than before. For he who has not become good even by being well treated, deserves all the bitterer punishment. Since, then, this excuse of thine has been shown to be weak, and not only fails to save those who take refuge in it, but exposes them so much the more, we must provide ourselves with some other means of safety.

Basil: Tell me of what nature is that? since, as for me, I am at present scarce master of myself, you hast reduced me to such a state of fear and trembling by what you hast said.

Chrysostom: Do not, I beseech and implore you, do not be so downcast. For while there is safety for us who are weak, namely, in not undertaking this office at

all, there is safety for you too who are strong, and this
consists in making your hopes of salvation depend, next
to the grace of God, on avoiding every act unworthy of
this gift, and of God who gave it. For they certainly would
be deserving of the greatest punishment who, after
obtaining this dignity through their own ambition, should
then either on account of sloth, or wickedness, or even
inexperience, abuse the office. Not that we are to gather
from this that there is pardon in store for those who have
not been thus ambitious. Yea, even they too are deprived
of all excuse. For in my judgment, if ten thousand were to
entreat and urge, a man should pay them no attention, but
should first of all search his own heart and examine the
whole matter carefully before yielding to their
importunities. Now no one would venture to undertake
the building of a house were he not an architect, nor will
anyone attempt the cure of sick bodies who is not a
skilled physician; but even though many urge him, will
beg off, and will not be ashamed to own his ignorance;
and shall he who is going to have the care of so many
souls entrusted to him, not examine himself beforehand?
will he accept this ministry even though he be the most
inexperienced of men, because this one commands him,
or that man constrains him, or for fear of offending a
third? And if so, how will he escape casting himself
together with them into manifest misery. Had he
continued as he was, it was possible for him to be saved,
but now he involves others in his own destruction. For
whence can he hope for salvation? whence to obtain
pardon? Who will then successfully intercede for us? they
who are now perhaps urging us and forcibly dragging us
on? But who will save these same at such a moment? For
even they too will stand in need in their turn of

intercession, that they may escape the fire. Now, that I say not these things to frighten you, but as representing the matter as in truth it is, hear what the holy Apostle Paul saith to Timothy his disciple, his own and beloved son, "Lay hands suddenly on no man, neither be partaker of other men's sins." Do you not see from what great blame, yea and vengeance, we, so far as in us lies, have delivered those who were ready to put us forward for this office.

2. For as it is not enough for those who are chosen to say in excuse for themselves, "I did not summon myself to this office, nor could I avoid what I did not see beforehand;" so neither will it be a sufficient plea for those who ordain them to say that they did not know him who was ordained. The charge against them becomes greater on account of their ignorance of him whom they brought forward, and what seems to excuse them only serves to accuse them the more. For how absurd a thing, is it not? that they who want to buy a slave, show him to the physician, and require sureties for the sale, and information about him from their neighbors, and after all this do not yet venture on his purchase without asking for some time for a trial of him; while they who are going to admit any one to so great an office as this, give their testimonial and their sanction loosely and carelessly, without further investigation, just because someone wishes it, or to court the favor, or to avoid the displeasure of someone else. Who shall then successfully intercede for us in that day, when they who ought to defend us stand themselves in need of defenders? He who is going to ordain, therefore, ought to make diligent inquiry, and much more he who is to be ordained. For though they who ordain him share his punishment, for any sins which he may commit in his office, yet so far from escaping

vengeance he will even pay a greater penalty than they— save only if they who chose him acted from some worldly motive contrary to what seemed justifiable to themselves. For if they should be detected so doing and knowing a man to be unworthy have brought him forward on some pretext or other, the amount of their punishment shall be equivalent to his, nay perhaps the punishment shall be even greater for them who appointed the unfit man. For he who gives authority to anyone who is minded to destroy the Church, would be certainly to blame for the outrages which that person commits. But if he is guilty of no such thing and says that he has been misled by the opinions of others, even then he shall not altogether remain unpunished, but his punishment shall be a little lighter than his who has been ordained. What then? It is possible that they who elect may come to the election deceived by a false report. But he who is elected could not say, "I am ignorant of myself," as others were of him. As one who will receive therefore a sorer punishment than they who put him forward, so should he make his scrutiny of himself more careful than that which they make of him; and if they in ignorance drag him on, he ought to come forward and instruct them carefully about any matters whereby he may stop their being misled; and so having shown himself unworthy of trial may escape the burden of so high an office.

For what is the reason why, in the arts of war, and merchandize, and husbandry, and other departments of this life, when some plan is proposed, the husbandman will not undertake to navigate the ship, nor the soldier to till the ground, nor the pilot to lead an army, under pain of ten thousand deaths? Is it not plainly this? that each foresees the danger which would attend his incompetence? Well, where the loss is concerned with trifles shall we use so much forethought, and refuse to yield to the pressure of compulsion, but where the punishment is eternal, as it is for those who know not how to handle the Priesthood, shall we want only and inconsiderately run into so great danger, and then advance, as our excuse, the pressing entreaties of others? But He who one day will judge us will entertain no such plea as this. For we ought to show far more caution in spiritual matters than in carnal. But now we are not found exhibiting as much caution. For tell me: if supposing a man to be an artificer, when he is not so, we invited him to do a piece of work, and he were to respond to the call, and then having set his hand to the material prepared for the building, were to spoil the wood and spoil the stone, and so to build the house that it straightway fell to pieces, would it be sufficient excuse for him to allege that he had been urged by others and did not come of his own accord? in no wise; and very reasonably and justly so. For he ought to have refused even at the call of others. So, for the man who only spoils wood and stone, there will be no escape from paying the penalty, and is he who destroys souls, and builds the temple of God carelessly, to think that the compulsion of others is his warrant for escaping punishment? Is not this very absurd? For I omit the fact as yet that no one is able to compel the man who is unwilling. But be it that he was subjected to excessive pressure and divers artful devices, and then fell into a snare; will this therefore rescue him from punishment? I beseech you, let us not deceive ourselves, and pretend that we know not what is obvious to a mere child. For surely this pretense of ignorance will not be able to profit in the day of reckoning. You were not ambitious, you sayest, of receiving this high office, conscious of thine own weakness. Well and good. Then you ought, with the same mind, to have declined the solicitation of others; or, when no one called you, was you weak and incapable, but when those were found ready to offer you this dignity, didst you suddenly become competent? What ludicrous nonsense! worthy of the extremist punishment. For this reason, also the Lord counsels the man who wishes to build a tower, not to lay the foundation before he has taken his own ability to build into account, lest he should give the passersby innumerable opportunities of mocking at him. But in his case the penalty only consists in becoming a laughingstock; while in that before us the punishment is that of fire unquenchable, and of an undying worm, gnashing of teeth, outer darkness, and being cut asunder, and having a portion with the hypocrites. But my accusers are unwilling to consider any of these things. For otherwise they would cease to blame a person who is unwilling to perish without cause. It is not the management of corn and barley, oxen or sheep, that is now under our consideration, nor any such like matters, but the very Body of Jesus. For the Church of Christ, according to St. Paul, is Christ's Body, and he who is entrusted with its care ought to train it up to a state of healthiness, and beauty unspeakable, and to look everywhere, lest any spot or wrinkle, or other like blemish should mar its vigor and comeliness. For what is this but to make it appear worthy, so far as human power can, of the incorruptible and ever-blessed Head which is set over it? If they who are ambitious of reaching an athletic condition of body need the help of physicians and trainers, and exact diet, and constant exercise, and a thousand other rules (for the omission of the merest trifle upsets and spoils the whole), how shall they to whose lot falls the care of the body, which has its conflict not against flesh and blood, but against powers unseen, be able to keep it sound and healthy, unless they far surpass ordinary human virtue, and are versed in all healing proper for the soul?

3. Pray, art you not aware that that body is subject to more diseases and assaults than this flesh of ours, is more quickly corrupted, and more slow to recover? and by those who have the healing of these bodies, divers medicines have been discovered, and an apparatus of different instruments, and diet suitable for the sick; and often the condition of the atmosphere is of itself enough for the recovery of a sick man; and there are instances of seasonable sleep having saved the physician all further labor. But in the case before us, it is impossible to take any of these things into consideration; nay there is but one method and way of healing appointed, after we have gone wrong, and that is, the powerful application of the Word. This is the one instrument, the only diet, the finest atmosphere. This takes the place of physic, cautery and cutting, and if it be needful to sear and amputate, this is the means which we must use, and if this be of no avail, all else is wasted; with this we both rouse the soul when it sleeps, and reduce it when it is inflamed; with this we cut off excesses, and fill up defects, and perform all manner of other operations which are requisite for the soul's health. Now as regards the ordering of our daily life for the best, it is true that the life of another may provoke us to emulation. But in the matter of spurious doctrine, when any soul is diseased thereby, then there is great need of the Word, not only in view of the safety of our own people, but in view of the enemy without. If, indeed, one

had the sword of the spirit, and the shield of faith, so as to be able to work miracles, and by means of these marvels to stop the mouths of impudent gainsayers, one would have little need of the assistance of the Word; still in the days of miracles the Word was by no means useless, but essentially necessary. For St. Paul made use of it himself, although he was everywhere so great an object of wonder for his miracles; and another of those who belonged to the "glorious company of the Apostles" exhorts us to apply ourselves to acquiring this power, when he says: "Be ready always to give an answer to every man that asks you a reason concerning the hope that is in you," and they all, with one accord, committed the care of the poor widows to Stephen, for no other reason than that they themselves might have leisure "for the ministry of the Word." To this we ought equally to apply ourselves, unless indeed we are endued with a power of working miracles. But if there is not the least sign of such a power being left us, while on every side many enemies are constantly attacking us, why then it necessarily follows that we should arm ourselves with this weapon, both in order that we may not be wounded ourselves with the darts of the enemy, and in order that we may wound him.

4. Wherefore it should be our ambition that the Word of Christ dwell in us richly. For it is not for one kind of battle only that we have to be prepared. This warfare is manifold, and is engaged with a great variety of enemies; neither do all these use the same weapons, nor do they practice the same method of attack; and he who has to join battle with all, must needs know the artifices of all, and be at once both archer and slinger, captain and general, in the ranks and in command, on foot and on horseback, in sea-fight and in siege. In common warfare,

indeed, each man repels the enemy by discharging the particular duty which he has undertaken. But here it is otherwise; and if anyone wishes to come off conqueror in this warfare, he must understand all forms of the art, as the devil knows well how to introduce his own assailants through any one spot which may happen to be unguarded, and to carry off the sheep. But not so where he perceives the shepherd coming equipped with accurate knowledge at all points, and well acquainted with his plotting. Wherefore we ought to be well-guarded in all parts: for a city, so long as it happens to be surrounded with a wall, laughs to scorn the besiegers, abiding in great security; but if anyone makes a breach in the wall, though but of the size of a gate, the rest of the circuit is of no use, although the whole of it stand quite securely; so it is with the city of God: so long as the presence of mind and wisdom of the shepherd, which answers to the wall, protect it on all sides, all the enemy's devices end in his confusion and ridicule, and they who dwell within the wall abide unmolested, but wherever any one has been able to demolish a single part, though the rest stand never so fast, through that breach ruin will enter upon the whole. For to what purpose does a man contend earnestly with the Greeks, if at the same time he becomes a prey to the Jews? or get the better of both these and then fall into the clutches of the Manicheans? or after he has proved himself superior to them even, if they who introduce fatalism enter in, and make havoc of the flock? But not to enumerate all the heresies of the devil, it will be enough to say that unless the shepherd is well skilled in refuting them all, the wolf, by means of any one of them, can enter, and devour the greater part of the flock. In ordinary warfare we must always look for victory being won or defeat sustained by the soldiers who are on the field of battle. But in the spiritual warfare the case is quite different. For there it often happens that the combat with one set of enemies secures a victory for others who never engaged in battle at all, nor took any trouble, but were sitting still all the while; and he who has not much experience in such occurrences will get pierced, so to say, with his own sword, and become the laughing-stock of friends and foes alike. I will try by an example to make clear what I am saying. They who receive the wild doctrines of Valentinus and Marcion, and of all whose minds are similarly diseased, exclude the Law given by God to Moses from the catalogue of the Divine Scriptures. But Jews so revere the Law, that although the time has come which annuls it, they still contend for the observance of all its contents, contrary to the purpose of God. But the Church of God, avoiding either extreme, has trodden a middle path, and is neither induced on the one hand to place herself under its yoke, nor on the other does she tolerate its being slandered, but commends it, though its day is over, because of its profitableness while its season lasted. Now it is necessary for him who is going to fight with both these enemies, to be fully conversant with this middle course. For if in wishing to teach the Jews that they are out of date in clinging to the old law, he begins to find fault with it unsparingly, he gives no little handle to those heretics who wish to pull it to pieces; and if in his ambition to stop their mouths he extols it immoderately, and speaks of it with admiration, as necessary for this present time, he unseals the lips of the Jews. Again, they who labor under the frenzy of Sabellius and the craze of Arius, have both fallen from a sound faith for want of observing a middle course. The name of Christian is applied to both these heretics; but if anyone examines their doctrines, he will find the one sect not much better than the Jews, and differing from them only in name, and the other very nearly holding the heresy of Paul of Samosata, and that both are very wide of the truth. Great, therefore, is the danger in such cases, and the way of orthodoxy is narrow and hemmed in by threatening crags on either side, and there is no little fear lest when intending to strike at one enemy we should be wounded by the other. For if any one assert the unity of the Godhead, Sabellius straightway turns that expression to the advantage of his own mental vagary, and if he distinguish the Persons, and say that the Father is one, and the Son another, and the Holy Spirit a third, up gets Arius, ready to wrest that distinction of Persons into a difference of substance; so we must turn and flee both from the impious confounding of the Persons by the one, and the senseless division of the substance by the other, confessing, indeed, that the Godhead of the Father and of the Son and of the Holy Ghost, is all one, while we add thereunto a Trinity of Persons. For then we shall be able to fortify ourselves against the attacks of both heretics. I might tell you besides these, of several other adversaries against which, except we contend bravely and carefully, we shall leave the field covered with wounds.

5. Why should anyone describe the silly chatter of our own people? For these are not less than the attacks upon us from without, while they give the teacher even more trouble. Some out of an idle curiosity are rashly bent upon busying themselves about matters which are neither possible for them to know, nor of any advantage to them if they could know them. Others again demand from God an account of his judgments and force themselves to

sound the depth of that abyss which is unfathomable. "For thy judgments," saith the Scriptures, "are a great deep," and about their faith and practice you would find few of them anxious, but the majority curiously inquiring into matters which it is not possible to discover, and the mere inquiry into which provokes God. For when we make a determined effort to learn what He does not wish us to know, we fail to succeed (for how should we succeed against the will of God?); and there only remains for us the danger arising from our inquiry. Now, though this be the case, whenever anyone authoritatively stops the search, into such fathomless depths, he gets himself the reputation of being proud and ignorant; so that at such times much tact is needed on the Bishop's part, so as to lead his people away from these unprofitable questions, and himself escape the above-named censures. In short, to meet all these difficulties, there is no help given but that of speech, and if any be destitute of this power, the souls of those who are put under his charge (I mean of the weaker and more meddlesome kind) are no better off than ships continually storm-tossed. So that the Priest should do all that in him lies, to gain this means of strength.

6. Basil: "Why, then, was not St. Paul ambitious of becoming perfect in this art? He makes no secret of his poverty of speech, but distinctly confesses himself to be unskilled, even telling the Corinthians so, who were admired for their eloquence, and prided themselves upon it."

Chrysostom: This is the very thing which has ruined many and made them remiss in the study of true doctrine. For while they failed to fathom the depths of the apostle's mind, and to understand the meaning of his words, they passed all their time slumbering and yawning, and paying respect not to that ignorance which St. Paul acknowledges, but to a kind from which he was as free as any man ever was in the world.

But leaving this subject to await our consideration, I say this much in the meantime. Granting that St. Paul was in this respect as unskilled as they would have him to be, what has that to do with the men of to-day? For he had a greater power by far than power of speech, power which brought about greater results too, which was that his bare presence, even though he was silent, was terrible to the demons. But the men of the present day, if they were all collected in one place, would not be able, with infinite prayers and tears, to do the wonders that once were done by the handkerchief of St. Paul. He too by his prayers raised the dead, and wrought such other miracles, that he was held to be a god by heathen; and before he was removed from this life, he was thought worthy to be caught up as far as the third heaven, and to share in such converse as it is not lawful for mortal ears to hear. But the men of to-day—not that I would say anything harsh or severe, for indeed I do not speak by way of insult to them, but only in wonder—how is it that they do not shudder when they measure themselves with so great a man as this? For if we leave the miracles and turn to the life of this blessed saint, and look into his angelic conversation, it is in this rather than in his miracles that you will find this Christian athlete a conqueror. For how can one describe his zeal and forbearance, his constant perils, his continual cares, and incessant anxiety for the Churches, his sympathy with the weak, his many afflictions, his unwonted persecutions, his deaths daily? Where is the spot in the world, where is the continent or sea, that is a stranger to the labors of this righteous man? Even the desert has known his presence, for it often sheltered him in time of danger. For he underwent every species of attack, and achieved every kind of victory, and there was never any end to his contests and his triumphs.

Yet, all unawares, I have been led to do this man an injury. For his exploits are beyond all powers of description, and beyond mine in particular, just as the masters of eloquence surpass me. Nevertheless, since that holy apostle will judge us, not by the issue, but by the motive, I shall not forbear till I have stated one more circumstance which surpasses anything yet mentioned, as much as he himself surpasses all his fellow men. And what is this? After so many exploits, after such a multitude of victories, he prayed that he might go into hell, and be handed over to eternal punishment, if so be that those Jews, who had often stoned him, and done what they could to make away with him, might be saved, and come over to Christ. Now who so longed for Christ? If, indeed, his feelings towards him ought not to be described as something nobler than longing; shall we then any more compare ourselves with this saint, after so great grace was imparted to him from above, after so great virtue was manifested in himself? What could be more presumptuous?

Now, that he was not so unskilled, as some count him to be, I shall try to show in what follows. The unskilled person in men's estimation is not only one who is unpracticed in the tricks of profane oratory, but the man who is incapable of contending for the defense of the right faith, and they are right. But St. Paul did not say that he was unskilled in both these respects, but in one only; and in support of this he makes a careful distinction, saying that he was "rude in speech, but not in knowledge." Now were I to insist upon the polish of Isocrates, the weight of Demosthenes, the dignity of Thucydides, and the sublimity of Plato, in any one bishop, St. Paul would be strong evidence against me. But I pass by all such matters and the elaborate ornaments of profane oratory; and I take no account of style or of delivery; yea let a man's diction be poor and his composition simple and unadorned, but let him not be unskilled in the knowledge and accurate statement of doctrine; nor in order to screen his own sloth, deprive that holy apostle of the greatest of his gifts, and the sum of his praises.

7. For how was it, tell me, that he confounded the Jews which dwelt at Damascus, though he had not yet begun to work miracles? How was it that he wrestled with the Grecians and threw them? and why was he sent to Tarsus? Was it not because he was so mighty and victorious in the word, and brought his adversaries to such a pass that they, unable to brook their defeat, were provoked to seek his life? At that time, as I said, he had not begun to work miracles, nor could anyone say that the masses looked upon him with astonishment on account of any glory belonging to his mighty works, or that they who contended with him were overpowered by the force of public opinion concerning him. For at this time he conquered by dint of argument only. How was it, moreover, that he contended and disputed successfully with those who tried to Judaize in Antioch? and how was it that that Areopagite, an inhabitant of Athens, that most devoted of all cities to the gods, followed the apostle, he and his wife? was it not owing to the discourse which they heard? And when Eutychus fell from the lattice, was it not owing to his long attendance even until midnight to St. Paul's preaching? How do we find him employed at

Thessalonica and Corinth, in Ephesus and in Rome itself? Did he not spend whole nights and days in interpreting the Scriptures in their order? and why should anyone recount his disputes with the Epicureans and Stoics. For were we resolved to enter into every particular, our story would grow to an unreasonable length.

When, therefore, both before working miracles, and after, St. Paul appears to have made much use of argument, how can anyone dare to pronounce him unskillful whose sermons and disputations were so exceedingly admired by all who heard them? Why did the Lycaonians imagine that he was Hermes? The opinion that he and Barnabas were gods indeed, arose out of the sight of their miracles; but the notion that he was Hermes did not arise from this, but was a consequence of his speech. In what else did this blessed saint excel the rest of the apostles? and how comes it that up and down the world he is so much on every one's tongue? How comes it that not merely among ourselves, but also among Jews and Greeks, he is the wonder of wonders? Is it not from the power of his epistles? whereby not only to the faithful of to-day, but from his time to this, yea and up to the end, even the appearing of Christ, he has been and will be profitable, and will continue to be so as long as the human race shall last. For as a wall built of adamant, so his writings fortify all the Churches of the known world, and he as a most noble champion stands in the midst, bringing into captivity every thought to the obedience of Christ, casting down imaginations, and every high thing which exalts itself against the knowledge of God, and all this he does by those epistles which he has left to us full of wonders and of Divine wisdom. For his writings are not only useful to us, for the overthrow of false doctrine and the confirmation of the true, but they help not a little towards living a good life. For by the use of these, the bishops of the present day fit and fashion the chaste virgin, which St. Paul himself espoused to Christ, and conduct her to the state of spiritual beauty; with these, too, they drive away from her the noisome pestilences which beset her, and preserve the good health thus obtained. Such are the medicines and such their efficacy left us by this so-called unskillful man, and they know them and their power best who constantly use them. From all this it is evident that St. Paul had given himself to the study of which we have been speaking with great diligence and zeal.

8. Hear also what he says in his charge to his disciple: "Give heed to reading, to exhortation, to teaching," and he goes on to show the usefulness of this by adding, "For in doing this you shalt save both thyself and them that hear you." And again he says, "The Lord's servant must not strive, but be gentle towards all, apt to teach, forbearing;" and he proceeds to say, "But abide you in the things which you hast learned, and hast been assured of, knowing of whom you hast learned them, and that from a babe you hast known the sacred writings which are able to make you wise unto salvation," and again, "Every Scripture is inspired of God, and also profitable for teaching, for reproof, for correction, for instruction which is in righteousness, that the man of God may be complete." Hear what he adds further in his directions to Titus about the appointment of bishops. "The bishop," he says, "must be holding to the faithful word which is according to the teaching, that he may be able to convict the gainsayers." But how shall anyone who is unskillful as these men pretend, be able to convict the

gainsayers and stop their mouths? or what need is there to give attention to reading and to the Holy Scriptures, if such a state of unskillfulness is to be welcome among us? Such arguments are mere makeshifts and pretexts, the marks of idleness and sloth. But someone will say, "it is to the priests that these charges are given:"—certainly, for they are the subjects of our discourse. But that the apostle gives the same charge to the laity, hear what he says in another epistle to other than the priesthood: "Let the word of Christ dwell in you richly in all wisdom," and again, "Let your speech be always with grace seasoned with salt, that ye may know how ye ought to answer each one," and there is a general charge to all that they "be ready to" render an account of their faith, and to the Thessalonians, he gives the following command: "Build each other up, even as also ye do." But when he speaks of priests he says, "Let the elders that rule well be counted worthy of double honor, especially those who labor in the word, and in teaching." For this is the perfection of teaching when the teachers both by what they do, and by what they say as well, bring their disciples to that blessed state of life which Christ appointed for them. For example, alone is not enough to instruct others. Nor do I say this of myself; it is our Savior's own word. "For whosoever shall do and teach them, he shall be called great. Now if doing were the same as teaching, the second word here would be superfluous; and it had been enough to have said "whosoever shall do" simply. But now by distinguishing the two, he shows that practice is one thing, and doctrine another, and that each needs the help of the others in order to complete edification. You hear too what the chosen vessel of Christ says to the Ephesian elders: "Wherefore watch ye, remembering that for the space of three years, I ceased not to admonish every one, night and day, with tears." But what need was there for his tears or for admonition by word of mouth, while his life as an apostle was so illustrious? His holy life might be a great inducement to men to keep the commandments, yet I dare not say that it alone could accomplish everything.

9. But when a dispute arises concerning matters of doctrine, and all take their weapons from the same Scriptures, of what weight will any one's life be able to prove? What then will be the good of his many austerities, when after such painful exercises, any one from the Priest's great unskillfulness in argument fall into heresy and be cut off from the body of the Church, a misfortune which I have myself seen many sufferings. Of what profit then will his patience be to him? None; no more than there will be in a sound faith if the life is corrupt. Wherefore, for this reason more than for all others, it concerns him whose office it is to teach others, to be experienced in disputations of this kind. For though he himself stands safely, and is unhurt by the gainsayers, yet the simple multitude under his direction, when they see their leader defeated, and without any answer for the gainsayers, will be apt to lay the blame of his discomfiture not on his own weakness, but on the doctrines themselves, as though they were faulty; and so by reason of the inexperience of one, great numbers are brought to extreme ruin; for though they do not entirely go over to the adversary, yet they are forced to doubt about matters in which formerly they firmly believed, and those whom they used to approach with unswerving confidence, they are unable to hold to any longer steadfastly, but in consequence of their leader's defeat, so great a storm settles down upon their souls, that the

mischief ends in their shipwreck altogether. But how dire is the destruction, and how terrible the fire which such a leader brings upon his own wretched head for every soul which is thus lost, you will not need to learn from me, as you know all this perfectly. Is this then pride, is this vainglory in me, to be unwilling to be the cause of the destruction of so many souls? and of procuring for myself greater punishment in the world to come, than that which now awaits me there? Who would say so? surely no one, unless he should wish to find fault where there is none, and to moralize over other men's calamities.

Book V.

1. How great is the skill required for the teacher in contending earnestly for the truth, has been sufficiently set forth by us. But I have to mention one more matter beside this, which is a cause of numberless dangers, though for my own part I should rather say that the thing itself is not the cause, but they who know not how to use it rightly, since it is of itself a help to salvation and to much good besides, whenever you finds that earnest and good men have the management of it. What then, do I mean by this? The expenditure of great labor upon the preparation of discourses to be delivered in public. For to begin with, the majority of those who are under the preachers' charge are not minded to behave towards them as towards teachers, but disdaining the part of learners, they assume instead the attitude of those who sit and look on at the public games; and just as the multitude there is separated into parties, and some attach themselves to one, and some to another, so here also men are divided, and become the partisans now of this teacher, now of that,

listening to them with a view to favor or spite. And not only is there this hardship, but another quite as great. For if it has occurred to any preacher to weave into his sermons any part of other men's works, he is exposed to greater disgrace than those who steal money. Nay, often where he has not even borrowed anything from anyone, but is only suspected, he has suffered the fate of a thief. And why do I speak of the works of others when it is not permitted to him to use his own resources without variety? For the public are accustomed to listen not for profit, but for pleasure, sitting like critics of tragedies, and of musical entertainments, and that facility of speech against which we declaimed just now, in this case becomes desirable, even more than in the case of barristers, where they are obliged to contend one against the other. A preacher then should have loftiness of mind, far exceeding my own littleness of spirit, that he may correct this disorderly and unprofitable pleasure on the part of the multitude, and be able to lead them over to a more useful way of hearing, that his people may follow and yield to him, and that he may not be led away by their own humors, and this it is not possible to arrive at, except by two means: indifference to their praise, and the power of preaching well.

2. For if either of these be lacking, the remaining one becomes useless, owing to its divorce from the other, for if a preacher be indifferent to praise, and yet cannot produce the doctrine "which is with grace seasoned with salt," he becomes despised by the multitude, while he gains nothing from his own nobleness of mind; and if on the other hand he is successful as a preacher, and is overcome by the thought of applause, harm is equally done in turn, both to himself and the multitude, because in

his desire for praise he is careful to speak rather with a view to please than to profit. And as he who neither lets good opinion influence him, nor is skillful in speaking, does not yield to the pleasure of the multitude, and is unable to do them any good worth mentioning, because he has nothing to say, so he who is carried away with desire for praise, though he is able to render the multitude better service, rather provides in place of this such food as will suit their taste, because he purchases thereby the tumult of acclamation.

3. The best kind of Bishop must, therefore, be strong in both these points, so that neither may supplant the other. For if when he stands up in the congregation and speaks words calculated to make the careless wince, he then stumbles, and stops short, and is forced to blush at his failure, the good of what he has spoken is immediately wasted. For they who are rebuked, being galled by what has been told them, and unable to avenge themselves on him otherwise, taunt him, with jeers at this ignorance of his, thinking to screen their own reproach thereby. Wherefore he ought, like some very good charioteer, to come to an accurate judgment about both these good things, in order that he may be able to deal with both as he may have need; for when he is irreproachable in the eyes of all, then he will be able, with just so much authority as he wishes, both to correct and to remit from correction all those who are under his rule. But without this it will not be easy for him to do so. But this nobleness of soul should be shown not only up to the limit of indifference to praise but should go further in order that the gain thus gotten may not in its turn be fruitless.

4. To what else ought he then to be indifferent? Slander and envy. Unseasonable evil speaking, however

(for of course the Bishop undergoes some groundless censure), it is well that he should neither fear nor tremble at excessively, nor entirely pass over; but we ought, though it happens to be false, or to be brought against us by the common herd, to try and extinguish it immediately. For nothing so magnifies both an evil and a good report as the undisciplined mob. For accustomed to hear and to speak without stopping to make inquiry, they repeat at random everything which comes in their way, without any regard to the truth of it. Therefore, the Bishop ought not to be unconcerned about the multitude, but straightway to nip their evil surmising in the bud; persuading his accusers, even if they be the most unreasonable of all men, and to omit nothing which is able to dispel an ill-favored report. But if, when we do all this, they who blame us will not be persuaded, thenceforward we should give them no concern. Since if anyone be too quick to be dejected by these accidents, he will not be able at any time to produce anything noble and admirable. For despondency and constant cares are mighty for destroying the powers of the mind, and for reducing it to extreme weakness. Thus then must the Priest behave towards those in his charge, as a father would behave to his very young children; and as such are not disturbed either by their insults or their blows, or their lamentations, nor even if they laugh and rejoice with us, do we take much account of it; so should we neither be puffed up by the promises of these persons nor cast down at their censure, when it comes from them unseasonably. But this is hard, my good friend; and perhaps, methinks, even impossible. For I know not whether any man ever succeeded in the effort not to be pleased when he is praised, and the man who is pleased at this is likely also to desire to enjoy it, and the man who desires to enjoy it will, of necessity, be altogether vexed and beside himself whenever he misses it. For as they who revel in being rich, when they fall into poverty are grieved, and they who have been used to live luxuriously cannot bear to live shabbily; so, too, they who long for applause, not only when they are blamed without a cause, but when they are not constantly being praised, become, as by some famine, wasted in soul, particularly when they happen themselves to have been used to praise, or if they hear others being praised. He who enters upon the trial of preaching with desires of this kind, how many annoyances and how many pangs dost you think that he has? It is no more possible for the sea to be without waves than that man to be without cares and grief.

5. For though the preacher may have great ability (and this one would only find in a few), not even in this case is he released from perpetual toil. For since preaching does not come by nature, but by study, suppose a man to reach a high standard of it, this will then forsake him if he does not cultivate his power by constant application and exercise. So that there is greater labor for the wiser than for the unlearned. For there is not the same degree of loss attending negligence on the part of the one and the other, but the loss is in exact proportion to the difference between the two possessions. For the latter no one would blame, as they furnish nothing worth regarding. But the former, unless they are constantly producing matter beyond the reputation in which all hold them, great censure attends on all hands; and besides these things, the latter would meet with considerable praise, even for small performances, while the efforts of the former, unless they be specially wonderful and startling, not only fail to win applause, but meet with

many fault-finders. For the audience set themselves to be critics, not so much in judgment of what is said as of the reputation of the speaker, so that whenever anyone excels all others in oratorical powers, then especially of all others does he need laborious study. For this man is not allowed to avail himself of the usual plea which human nature urges, that one cannot succeed in everything; but if his sermons do not throughout correspond to the greatness of the expectations formed, he will go away without having gained anything but countless jeers and censures; and no one takes this into consideration about him, that dejection and pain, and anxiety, and often anger, may step in, and dim the clearness of his thoughts and prevent his productions from coming from him unalloyed, and that on the whole, being but a man, he cannot be constantly the same, nor at all times acquit himself successfully, but naturally must sometimes fall short of the mark, and appear on a lower level of ability than usual. None of these things, as I said, are they willing to take into consideration, but charge him with faults as if they were sitting in judgment on an angel; though in other cases, too, a man is apt to overlook the good performances of his neighbor, though they be many and great, and if anywhere a defect appears, even if it be accidental, even if it only occur at long intervals, it is quickly perceived, and always remembered, and thus small and trifling matters have often lessened the glory of many and great doings.

6. You sees, my excellent friend, that the man who is powerful in preaching has peculiar need of greater study than others; and besides study, of forbearance also greater than what is needed by all those whom I have already mentioned. For thus are many constantly springing up against him, in a vain and senseless spirit,

and having no fault to find with him, but that he is generally approved of, hate him; and he must bear their bitter malice nobly, for as they are not able to hide this cursed hatred, which they so unreasonably entertain, they both revile, and censure, and slander in private, and defame in public, and the mind which has begun to be pained and exasperated, on every one of these occasions, will not escape being corrupted by grief. For they will not only revenge themselves upon him by their own acts but will try to do so by means of others, and often having chosen some one of those who are unable to speak a word, will extol him with their praises and admire him beyond his worth. Some do this through ignorance alone, some through ignorance and envy, in order that they may ruin the reputation of the other, not that they may prove the man to be wonderful who is not so, and the noble-minded man has not only to struggle against these, but often against the ignorance of the whole multitude; for since it is not possible that all those who come together should consist of learned men, but the chances are that the larger part of the congregation is composed of unlearned people, and that even the rest, who are clearer headed than they, fall as far short of being able to criticize sermons as the remainder again fall short of them; so that only one or two are seated there who possess this power; it follows, of necessity, that he who preaches better than others carries away less applause, and possibly goes home without being praised at all, and he must be prepared to meet such anomalies nobly, and to pardon those who commit them in ignorance, and to weep for those who acquiesce in them on account of envy as wretched and pitiable creatures, and not to consider that his powers have become less on either of these accounts. For if a man, being a pre-eminently good painter, and superior to all in his art, sees the portrait which he has drawn with great accuracy held up to ridicule, he ought not to be dejected, and to consider the picture poor, because of the judgment of the ignorant; as he would not consider the drawing that is really poor to be something wonderful and lovely, because of the astonishment of the inartistic.

7. For let the best artificer be himself the critic of his own designs, and let his performances be determined to be good or poor, according as the mind which designed them gives sentence upon them. But let him not even consider the opinion, so erroneous and inartistic, of the outside world. Let, therefore, the man who undertakes the strain of teaching never give heed to the good opinion of the outside world, nor be dejected in soul on account of such persons; but laboring at his sermons so that he may please God, (For let this alone be his rule and determination, in discharging this best kind of workmanship, not acclamation, nor good opinions,) if, indeed, he be praised by men, let him not repudiate their applause, and when his hearers do not offer this, let him not seek it, let him not be grieved. For a sufficient consolation in his labors, and one greater than all, is when he is able to be conscious of arranging and ordering his teaching with a view to pleasing God.

8. For if he be first carried away with the desire for indiscriminate praise, he will reap no advantage from his labors, or from his power in preaching, for the mind being unable to bear the senseless censures of the multitude is dispirited, and casts aside all earnestness about preaching. Therefore, it is especially necessary to be trained to be indifferent to all kinds of praise. For to know how to preach is not enough for the preservation of

that power, if this be not added: and if anyone would examine accurately the man who is destitute of this art, he will find that he needs to be indifferent to praise no less than the other, for he will be forced to do many wrong things in placing himself under the control of popular opinion. For not having the energy to equal those who are in repute for the quality of their preaching, he will not refrain from forming ill designs against them, from envying them, and from blaming them without reason, and from many such discreditable practices, but will venture everything, even if it be needful to ruin his own soul, for the sake of bringing down their fame to the level of his own insignificance. And in addition to this, he will leave off his exertions about his work; a kind of numbness, as it were, spreading itself over his mind. For much toil, rewarded by scanty praise, is sufficient to cast down a man who cannot despise praise, and put him into a deep lethargy, since the husbandman even when he spends time over some sorry piece of land, and is forced to till a rock, quickly desists from his work, unless he is possessed of much earnestness about the matter, or has a fear of famine impending over him. For if they who are able to speak with considerable power, need such constant exercise for the preservation of their talent, he who collects no materials at all, but is forced in the midst of his efforts to meditate; what difficulty, what confusion, what trouble will he experience, in order that he may be able at great labor to collect a few ideas! and if any of those clergy who are under his authority, and who are placed in the inferior order, be able in that position to appear to better advantage than he; what a divine mind must he have, so as not to be seized with envy or cast down by despondency. For, for one to be placed in a station of higher dignity, and to be surpassed by his inferior in rank, and to bear this nobly, would not be the part of any ordinary mind, nor of such as my own, but of one as hard as adamant; and if, indeed, the man who is in greater repute be very forbearing and modest, the suffering becomes so much the more easily borne. But if he is bold and boastful and vainglorious, a daily death would be desirable for the other; he will so embitter his life, insulting him to his face, and laughing at him behind his back, wresting much of his authority from him, and wishing to be everything himself. But he is possessed of the greatest security, in all these circumstances, who has fluency in preaching, and the earnest attention of the multitude about him, and the affection of all those who are under his charge. Dost not you know what a passion for sermons has burst in upon the minds of Christians now-a-days? and that they who practice themselves in preaching are in especial honor, not only among the heathen, but among them of the household of the faith? How then could anyone bear such disgrace as to find that all are mute when he is preaching, and think that they are oppressed, and wait for the end of the sermon, as for some release from work; while they listen to another with eagerness though he preach long, and are sorry when he is about to conclude; and almost angry when it is his purpose to be silent. If these matters seem to you to be small, and easily to be despised, it is because of thine inexperience. They are truly enough to quench zeal, and to paralyze the powers of the mind, unless a man withdraw himself from all human passions, and study to frame his conduct after the pattern of those incorporeal powers, who are neither pursued by envy, nor by longing for fame, nor by any other morbid feeling. If then there be any man so constituted as to be able to subdue this wild beast, so difficult to capture, so unconquerable, so fierce; that is to say, public fame, and to cut off its many heads, or rather to forbid their growth altogether; he will easily be able to repel these many violent assaults, and to enjoy a kind of quiet haven of rest. But he who has not freed himself from this monster, involves his soul in struggles of various kinds, and perpetual agitation, and the burden both of despondency and of other passions. But why need I detail the rest of these difficulties, which no one will be able to describe, or to learn unless he has had actual experience of them.

Book VI.

1. Our condition here, indeed, is such as you hast heard. But our condition hereafter how shall we endure, when we are compelled to give our account for each of those who have been entrusted to us? For our penalty is not limited to shame, but everlasting chastisement awaits us as well. As for the passage, "Obey them that have the rule over you, and submit to them, for they watch in behalf of your souls as they that shall give account;" though I have mentioned it once already, yet I will break silence about it now, for the fear of its warning is continually agitating my soul. For if for him who causes one only, and that the least, to stumble, it is profitable that "a great millstone should be hanged about his neck, and that he should be sunk in the depth of the sea;"200and if they who wound the consciences of the brethren, sin against Christ Himself, what then will they one day suffer, what kind of penalty will they pay, who destroy not one only, or two, or three, but so many multitudes?

For it is not possible for inexperience to be urged as an excuse, nor to take refuge in ignorance, nor for the plea of necessity or force to be put forward. Yea, if it were possible, one of those under their charge could more easily make use of this refuge for his own sins than bishops in the case of the sins of others. Do you ask why? Because he who has been appointed to rectify the ignorance of others, and to warn them beforehand of the conflict with the devil which is coming upon them, will not be able to put forward ignorance as his excuse, or to say, "I have never heard the trumpet sound, I did not foresee the conflict." For he is set for that very purpose, says Ezekiel, that he may sound the trumpet for others, and warn them of the dangers at hand. And therefore, his chastisement is inevitable, though he that perishes happen to be but one. "For if when the sword comes, the watchman does not sound the trumpet to the people, nor give them a sign, and the sword come and take any man away, he indeed is taken away on account of his iniquity, but his blood will I require at the watchman's hands."

    2. Cease then to urge us on to a penalty so inevitable; for our discourse is not about an army, or a kingdom; but about an office which needs the virtues of an angel. For the soul of the Priest ought to be purer than the very sunbeams, in order that the Holy Spirit may not leave him desolate, in order that he may be able to say, "Now I live; and yet no longer I, but Christ lives in me." For if they who dwell in the desert, and are removed far from the city and the market-place, and the tumult therein, and who enjoy all their time a haven of rest, and of peacefulness, are not willing to rely on the security of that manner of life, but add to it numberless other safeguards, hedging themselves round on every side, and studying

both to speak and to act with great circumspection, so that to the utmost extent of human power they may draw near to God with assurance, and with unstained purity, what power and strength, thinks you, does the ordained Priest need so as to be able to tear his soul away from every defilement, and to keep its spiritual beauty unsullied? For he has need of far greater purity than they; and whoever has need of greater purity, he too is subject to more pressing temptations than they, which are able to defile him, unless by using constant self-denial and much labor, he renders his soul inaccessible to them. For beauty of face, elegance of movement, an affected gait and lisping voice, penciled eyebrows and enameled cheeks, elaborate braiding and dyeing of hair, costliness of dress, variety of golden ornaments, and the glory of precious stones, the scent of perfumes, and all those other matters to which womankind devote themselves, are enough to disorder the mind, unless it happen to be hardened against them, through much austerity of self-restraint. Now to be disturbed indeed by such things is nothing wonderful. But on the other hand, that the devil should be able to hit and shoot down the souls of men by the opposite of these— this is a matter which fills us with astonishment and perplexity.

3. For ere now some men who have escaped these snares, have been caught by others widely differing from these. For even a neglected appearance, unkempt hair, squalid dress, and an unpainted face, simple behavior, and homely language, unstudied gait, and unaffected voice, a life of poverty, a despised, unpatronized and lonely condition, have first drawn on the beholder to pity, and next to utter ruin; and many who have escaped the former nets, in the way of gold ornaments and perfumes, and

apparel, and all the rest, of which I have spoken as connected with them, have easily fallen into these so widely differing from them, and have perished. When then both by poverty and by riches, both by the adornment and the neglect of the personal appearance, both by studied and unaffected manners, in short by all those means which I have enumerated, war is kindled in the soul of the beholder, and its artifices surround him on every side, how will he be able to breathe freely while so many snares encompass him? and what hiding-place will he be able to find—I do not say so as to avoid being forcibly seized by them (for this is not altogether difficult)—but so as to keep his own soul undisturbed by polluting thoughts?

And I pass by honors, which are the cause of countless evils. For those which come from the hands of women are ruinous to the vigor of self-restraint, and often overthrow it when a man does not know how to watch constantly against such designs; while those which come from the hands of men, unless a man receive them with much nobleness of mind, he is seized with two contrary emotions, servile flattery and senseless pride. To those who patronize him, he is obliged to cringe; and towards his inferiors he is puffed up, on account of the honors which the others confer, and is driven into the gulf of arrogance. We have mentioned these matters indeed, but how harmful they actually are, no one could well learn without experience. For not only these snares, but greater and more delusive than these, he must needs encounter, who has his conversation in the world. But he who is content with solitude, has freedom from all this, and if at any time a strange thought creates a representation of this kind, the image is weak, and capable of being speedily subdued, because there is no fuel added to the flame from without, arising from actual sight. For the recluse has but himself to fear for; or should he be forced to have the care of others they are easily counted: and if they be many, yet they are less than those in our Churches, and they give him who is set over them much lighter anxiety about them, not only on account of their fewness, but because they are all free from worldly concerns, and have neither wife nor children, nor any such thing to care about; and this makes them very deferential to their rulers, and allows them to share the same abode with them, so that they are able to take in their failings accurately at a glance and correct them, seeing that the constant supervision of a teacher is no little help towards advance in virtue.

4. But of those who are subject to the Priest, the greater number are hampered with the cares of this life, and this makes them the slower in the performance of spiritual duties. Whence it is necessary for the teacher to sow every day (so to speak), in order that by its frequency at least, the word of doctrine may be able to be grasped by those who hear. For excessive wealth, and an abundance of power, and sloth the offspring of luxury, and many other things beside these, choke the seeds which have been let fall. Often too the thick growth of thorns does not suffer the seed to drop even upon the surface of the soil. Again, excess of trouble, stress of poverty, constant insults, and other such things, the reverse of the foregoing, take the mind away from anxiety about things divine; and of their people's sins, not even the smallest part can become apparent; for how should it, in the case of those the majority of whom they do not know even by sight?

The Priest's relations with his people involve thus

much difficulty. But if any inquire about his relations with God, he will find the others to be as nothing, since these require a greater and more thorough earnestness. For he who acts as an ambassador on behalf of the whole city—but why do I say the city? on behalf of the whole world indeed—prays that God would be merciful to the sins of all, not only of the living, but also of the departed. What manner of man ought he to be? For my part I think that the boldness of speech of Moses and Elias, is insufficient for such supplication. For as though he were entrusted with the whole world and were himself the father of all men, he draws near to God, beseeching that wars may be extinguished everywhere, that tumults may be quelled; asking for peace and plenty, and a swift deliverance from all the ills that beset each one, publicly and privately; and he ought as much to excel in every respect all those on whose behalf he prays, as rulers should excel their subjects.

And whenever he invokes the Holy Spirit, and offers the most dread sacrifice, and constantly handles the common Lord of all, tell me what rank shall we give him? What great purity and what real piety must we demand of him? For consider what manner of hands they ought to be which minister in these things, and of what kind his tongue which utters such words, and ought not the soul which receives so great a spirit to be purer and holier than anything in the world? At such a time angels stand by the Priest; and the whole sanctuary, and the space round about the altar, is filled with the powers of heaven, in honor of Him who lieth thereon. For this, indeed, is capable of being proved from the very rites which are being then celebrated. I myself, moreover, have heard someone once relate, that a certain aged, venerable man, accustomed to see revelations, used to tell him, that he being thought worthy of a vision of this kind, at such a time, saw, on a sudden, so far as was possible for him, a multitude of angels, clothed in shining robes, and encircling the altar, and bending down, as one might see soldiers in the presence of their King, and for my part I believe it. Moreover another told me, without learning it from someone else, but as being himself thought worthy to be both an ear and eye witness of it, that, in the case of those who are about to depart hence, if they happen to be partakers of the mysteries, with a pure conscience, when they are about to breathe their last, angels keep guard over them for the sake of what they have received, and bear them hence. And dost you not yet tremble to introduce a soul into so sacred a mystery of this kind, and to advance to the dignity of the Priesthood, one robed in filthy raiment, whom Christ has shut out from the rest of the band of guests? The soul of the Priest should shine like a light beaming over the whole world. But mine has so great darkness overhanging it, because of my evil conscience, as to be always cast down and never able to look up with confidence to its Lord. Priests are the salt of the earth. But who would easily put up with my lack of understanding, and my inexperience in all things, but you, who hast been wont to love me beyond measure. For the Priest ought not only to be thus pure as one who has been dignified with so high a ministry, but very discreet, and skilled in many matters, and to be as well versed in the affairs of this life as they who are engaged in the world, and yet to be free from them all more than the recluses who occupy the mountains. For since he must mix with men who have wives, and who bring up children, who possess servants, and are surrounded with wealth, and fill public positions, and are persons of influence, he too should be a many-sided man—I say many-sided, not unreal, nor yet fawning and hypocritical, but full of much freedom and assurance, and knowing how to adapt himself profitably, where the circumstances of the case require it, and to be both kind and severe, for it is not possible to treat all those under one's charge on one plan, since neither is it well for physicians to apply one course of treatment to all their sick, nor for a pilot to know but one way of contending with the winds. For, indeed, continual storms beset this ship of ours, and these storms do not assail from without only, but take their rise from within, and there is need of much condescension, and circumspection, and all these different matters have one end in view, the glory of God, and the edifying of the Church.

5. Great is the conflict which recluses undergo, and much their toil. But if anyone compare their exertions with those which the right exercise of the Priesthood involves, he will find the difference as great as the distance between a king and a commoner. For there, if the labor is great indeed, yet the conflict is common to body and soul, or rather the greater part of it is accomplished by the condition of the body, and if this be not strong, the inclination remains undeveloped, and is unable to come out into action. For the habit of intense fasting, and sleeping on the ground, and keeping vigil, and refraining from the bath, and great toil, and all other means which they use for the affliction of the body are given up, when the body to be thus disciplined is not strong. But in this case purity of soul is the business in hand, and no bodily vigor is required to show its excellence. For what does strength of body contribute towards our being not self-

willed, or proud, or headstrong, but sober and prudent, and orderly, and all else, wherein St. Paul filled up the picture of the perfect Priest? But no one could say this of the virtues of the recluse.

6. But as in the case of wonderworkers, a large apparatus is required, both wheels and ropes and daggers; while the philosopher has the whole of his art stored up in his mind, not requiring any external appliances: So accordingly in the case before us. The recluse requires both a good condition of body, and a place suitable for his course of life, in order that such may not be settled too far from intercourse with their fellow men and may have the tranquility which belongs to desert places, and yet further, may not fail to enjoy the most favorable climate. For nothing is so unbearable to a body worn with fasting as a climate which is not equable. And what trouble they are compelled to take in the preparation of their clothing and daily food, as they are themselves ambitious of doing all with their own hands, I need not speak of now. But the Priest will require none of these things to supply his wants, but is unconcerned about them, and participates in all things which are harmless, while he has all his skill stored up in the treasure-house of his mind. But if anyone admire a solitary life, and retirement from the society of the multitude, I should say myself that such a life was a token of patience, but not a sufficient proof of entire fortitude of soul. For the man who sits at the helm in harbor, does not yet give any certain proof of his art. But if one is able to guide his ship safely in the midst of the sea, no one would deny him to be an excellent steersman.

7. It would be, therefore, in no wise excessively surprising to us, that the recluse, living as he does by himself, is undisturbed and does not commit many and

great sins. For he does not meet with things which irritate and excite his mind. But if anyone who has devoted himself to whole multitudes, and has been compelled to bear the sins of many, has remained steadfast and firm, guiding his soul in the midst of the storm as if he were in a calm, he is the man to be justly applauded and admired of all, for he has shown sufficient proof of personal manliness. Do not you, therefore, for thy part wonder if I, who avoid the marketplace and the haunts of the multitude, have not many to accuse me. For I ought not to wonder, if I sinned not when asleep, nor fell when I did not wrestle, nor was hit if I did not fight. For who, tell me, who will be able to speak against me, and reveal my depravity? Can this roof or cell? Nay, they would not be able to give tongue? Would my mother, who best of all knows my affairs? Well, certainly with her I am neither in communication, nor have we ever come to a quarrel, and if this had happened, no mother is so heartless and wanting in affection for her child as to revile and accuse before all him whom she travailed with, and brought forth, and reared, if there were no reason to constrain her, nor any person to urge her to such an act. Nevertheless, if anyone desires to make a careful inspection of my mind, he will discover much which is corrupt there. Nor art you unaware of this who art especially wont to extol me with praises before all. Now that I do not say these things out of mere modesty, recollect how often I said to you, when this subject was being discussed between us, "If any one were to give me my choice whether I would rather gain distinction in the oversight of the Church, or in the life of the recluse, I would vote a thousand times over for accepting the former. For I have never failed to congratulate those who have been able to discharge this office well, and no one will gainsay that what I counted blessed I would not have shunned were I able to take part in it fitly. But what am I to do? There is nothing so prejudicial to the oversight of the Church as this inactivity and negligence of mine, which others think to be a sort of self-discipline, but which I hold to be a veil as it were of my personal infirmity, covering the greater number of my defects and not suffering them to appear. For he who is accustomed to enjoy such great freedom from business, and to pass his time in much repose, even if he be of a noble nature, is confused by his inexperience, and is disturbed, and his inactivity deprives him of no small part of his natural ability. But when, besides, he is of slow intellect, and ignorant also of these severe trials, which I take it is my case, he will carry on this ministry which he has received no better than a statue. Wherefore of those who have come to such great trial, out of that school, few shine; and the greater part betray themselves, and fall, and undergo much hardship and sufferings; and no wonder. For the trials and the discipline are not concerned with the same things. The man who is contending in no wise differs from those who are untrained. He who thus enters this list should despise glory, be superior to anger, full of great discretion. But for the exercise of these qualities there is no scope in his case who affects a secluded life. For he does not have many to provoke him in order that he may practice chastising, the force of his anger: nor admirers and applauders in order that he may be trained to despise the praises of the multitudes. And of the discretion which is required in the Church, there is no taking account in their case. Whenever, therefore, they come to the trials of which they have never had practical experience, they get bewildered, their heads are turned, they fall into a state of helplessness, and besides adding nothing to their excellence, may have often lost that which they brought with them.

8. Basil: What then? shall we set over the administration of the Church those who move in society, and who are careful about the concerns of this world, who are adepts at wrangling and vituperation, are full of countless artifices, and versed in luxurious ways?

Chrysostom: Hush, dear friend that you are! You shouldest never entertain in thy thoughts such men as these, when the Priesthood is under discussion, but only such as are able after mixing and associating with all, to keep their purity undefiled, and their unworldliness, their holiness, constancy and sobriety unshaken, and to possess all other virtues which belong to recluses, in a greater degree than they. He who has many defects, but is able to hide them, by means of his seclusion, and to make them ineffectual, because he does not associate with any one, when he comes into society will gain nothing, but the position of a laughing-stock, and will run greater risks still, which I was very nearly experiencing myself, had not the providence of God quickly warded off such fire from my head. For it is not possible for one in such a position to escape notice when he is so conspicuously placed, but everything then is detected, and as the fire tests the material of metals, so too the trial of the clerical office searches the souls of mortal men; and if anyone be passionate or mean, or ambitious of fame, if he be boastful, or anything else of the kind, it unveils all; and speedily lays bare his defects, and not only lays them bare, but increases their painfulness and strength. For the wounds of the body, if they are galled, become harder to heal, and the emotions of the mind when chafed and irritated, are naturally more exasperated, and those who possess them are driven to commit greater sins. For they excite him who does not restrain them, to love of glory, and to boastfulness, and to desire for this world's goods, and draw him downwards, both to luxury and laxity of life, and to laziness, and, little by little, to evils worse than these which result from them. For many are the circumstances in society which have the power to upset the balance of the mind, and to hinder its straightforward course; and first of all is his social intercourse with women. For it is not possible for the Bishop, and one who is concerned with the whole flock, to have a care for the male portion of it, but to pass over the female, which needs more particular forethought, because of its propensity to sins. But the man who is appointed to the administration of a Bishopric must have a care for the moral health of these, if not in a greater, at least in no less a degree than the others. For it is necessary to visit them when they are sick, to comfort them when they are sorrowful, and to reprove them when they are idle, and to help them when they are distressed; and in such cases the evil one would find many opportunities of approach, if a man did not fortify himself with a very strict guard. For the eye, not only of the unchaste, but of the modest woman pierces and disturbs the mind. Flatteries enervate it, and favors enslave it, and fervent love—the spring one may say of all good—becomes the cause of countless evils to those who do not make a right use of it. Constant cares too have ere now blunted the edge of the understanding and have made that which was buoyant heavier than lead, while anger has burst in like smoke, and taken possession of all the inner man.

9. Why should anyone speak of the injuries that

result from grief, the insults, the abuse, the censure from superiors, from inferiors, from the wise, and from fools; for the class who are wanting in right judgment are particularly fond of censuring and will never readily allow any excuse. But the truly excellent Bishop ought neither to think lightly of these, but to clear himself with all men of the charges which they bring against him, with great forbearance and meekness, pardoning their unreasonable fault-finding, rather than being indignant and angry about it. For if St. Paul feared lest he should incur a suspicion of theft, among his disciples, and therefore procured others for the management of the money, that "no one" he says, "should blame us in this abundance which is administered by us," how ought we not to do all so as to remove evil suspicions, even if they happen to be false, and most unreasonable, and very foreign to our thought? For we are not so utterly removed from any sin as St. Paul from theft; notwithstanding, though so far from this evil practice, he did not, therefore, slight the suspicion of the world, although it was very absurd, and even insane. For it was madness to have any such suspicion about that blessed and admirable character. But none the less does he remove far off the causes of this suspicion, unreasonable though it was, and such as no one who was in his senses would entertain, and he neither disdained the folly of the multitudes, nor did he say, "To whose mind did it ever occur to suspect such things of us, after the signs which I have wrought, and the forbearance which has marked my life, and when you all revered and admired us?" Quite the contrary: he foresaw and expected this base suspicion, and pulled it up by the roots, or rather did not suffer it to grow at all. Why? "Because," saith he, "we provide things honest not only before the Lord, but before all men." So great, yea and far greater zeal must we use, to uproot and prevent floating reports which are not good, but to see beforehand from afar whence they come, and to remove beforehand the causes from which they are produced, not to wait till they are established and are the common topics in every one's mouth. For then it is not easy in the future to destroy them, but very difficult, perhaps impossible, and not without mischief, because this is done after many have been injured. But how far shall I continue pursuing the unattainable? For to enumerate all the difficulties in this direction, is nothing more nor less than measuring the ocean. Even when any one should clear himself from every passion (which is a thing impossible) in order to correct the failings of others, he is forced to undergo countless trials, and when his own infirmities are added, behold, an abyss of toil and care, and all that he must suffer, who wishes to subdue the evils in himself and in those around him.

10. Basil: And now, art you free from toils? Have you no cares while you live by yourself?

Chrysostom: I have indeed even now. For how is it possible for one who is a man, and who is living this toilsome life of ours, to be free from cares and conflict? But it is not quite the same thing for man to plunge into a boundless ocean and to cross a river, so great is the difference between these cares and those. For now, indeed, if I were able to become serviceable to others, I should wish it myself, and this would be a matter of prayer with me. But if it is not possible to help another, yet if it be practicable to save and rescue myself from the waves, I shall be contented.

Basil: Dost you then think this to be a great thing? and dost you fancy that you will be saved when you are not profitable to any other?

Chrysostom: You hast spoken well and nobly, for I am not myself able to believe that it is possible for one who has not labored for the salvation of his fellow to be saved, nor did it at all profit the wretched man in the Gospel that he had not diminished his talent; but he perished through not increasing it and bringing it doubled to his master. Nevertheless, I think that my punishment will be milder when I am called to account, because I have not saved others, than it would be if I should destroy myself and others too by becoming far worse after so great an honor. For now, I trust that my chastisement will be proportioned to the amount of my sins, but after receiving this office, I fear it would be not double, or threefold, but manifold, because I should have caused very many to stumble, and after additional honor should have offended the God who honored me.

11. For this very cause God accuses the Israelites more vehemently, and shows that they were worthy of greater chastisement, because they sinned after so many honors had come to them from Him, saying in one place: "But you only have I known of all the families of the earth, therefore will I punish you for your iniquities," and again, "and I raised up of your sons for prophets, and of your young men for Nazarites;" and before the times of the prophets, wishing to show that sins receive sorer punishment by far when they occur in the case of the Priest than in the case of the laity, He enjoins as great a sacrifice to be offered for the Priest as for the whole people,216 and this amounts to a proof on his part, that the wounds of the Priesthood need more assistance—that is, as great as those of all the people together, and they would not have needed a greater, except they were worse;

and they are not worse in their nature, but are aggravated through the dignity of the Priest, who dares to commit them. And why do I speak of the men who follow this ministration. For the daughters of the Priests, who have no part in the Priestly office, yet on account of their father's dignity undergo a far bitterer punishment for the same sins as others, and the offense is the same in their case and in the daughters of the laity; namely, fornication in both; yet the penalty is far severer for the former. Do you see with what abundant proof God shows you that he demands much greater punishment for the ruler than for the ruled? For no doubt he who punishes to a greater degree than others the daughter of a certain man for that man's sake, will not exact the same penalty from the man who is the cause of her additional chastisement as from others, but a much heavier one; and very reasonably; for the mischief does not merely involve himself, but it destroys the souls of the weaker brethren and of them who look up to him, and Ezekiel, writing to show this, distinguishes from one another the judgment of the rams and of the sheep.

12. Do we then seem to you to entertain a reasonable fear? for in addition to what has been said, although much toil is needful on my part, so that I should not be completely overwhelmed by the passions of my soul, yet I endure the toil, and I do not shun the conflict. For even now I am taken captive by vainglory, but I often recover myself, and I see at a glance that I have been taken, and there are times when I rebuke my soul, which has been enslaved; outrageous desires even now come over me, but they kindle only a languid flame, since my bodily eyes cannot fasten upon any fuel to feed the fire. From speaking ill of any, or from hearing any one evil

spoken of, I am utterly removed, since I have no one to talk with; for surely these walls would never give tongue; yet it is not altogether in like manner possible to avoid anger, although there be none to provoke it. For often when the recollection of outrageous men has come over me, and of the deeds done by them, it makes my heart swell. But not permanently, for I quickly subdue its kindling, and persuade it to be quiet, saying that it is very inexpedient and extremely despicable to leave one's own fault alone, and to busy oneself about the faults of one's neighbors. But were I to come among the multitude, and to be involved in countless excitements, I should not be able to have the benefit of this warning, nor to experience reflections which take me thus to task. But just as they who are driven over precipices by a torrent, or in some other way, are able to foresee the destruction to which they are finally going, and are unable to think of any means of help, so I, when I have fallen into the great tumult of my passions, shall be able to see at a glance my chastisement daily increasing. But to be master of myself as I am now, and to rebuke diseases of this sort raging on every side, would not be equally easy for me as it was before. For my soul is weak and puny, and easily mastered, not only by these passions, but by envy, which is bitterer than all of them. Neither does it know how to bear insults or honors temperately. But these do exceedingly elate it, while those depress it. As, then, savage wild beasts, when they are in good condition, and in full vigor, overcome those that fight with them, particularly, too, if they be feeble and unskillful; but if any one were to weaken them by starvation, he will put their rage to sleep, and will extinguish most of their strength; so that one, not over valiant, might take up the conflict and battle with them: so also with the passions of the soul. He who makes them weak, places them in subjection to right reason; but he who nourishes them carefully, makes his battle with them harder, and renders them so formidable that he passes all his time in bondage and fear.

What then is the food of these wild beasts? Of vainglory, indeed, it is honors and applause; of pride, abundance of authority and power; of envy, the reputation of one's neighbors; of avarice, the munificence of the generous; of incontinence, luxury and the constant society of women; and other passions have their proper nutriment? And all these things will sorely attack me if I come forth into the world, and will tear my soul to pieces, will be the more formidable and will make my battle with them the harder. Whereas, while I am established here, they will be subdued; and then, indeed, only with great exertion; yet at the same time, by the Grace of God, they will be subdued, and there will not be anything worse then than their bark. For these reasons I keep to this cell, and am inaccessible, self-contained, and unsociable, and I put up with hearing countless complaints of this kind, although I would gladly efface them, and have been vexed and grieved because I cannot; for it is not easy for me to become sociable, and at the same time to remain in my present security. Therefore, I beseech you, too, to pity rather than to censure one beset with such great difficulty.

But we cannot yet persuade you. Accordingly, the time is now come that I should utter to you the only thing which I have left unspoken. Perhaps it may seem to many to be incredible, but even so I shall not be ashamed to bring it before the world, for though what is said is proof of an evil conscience and of many sins, yet, since God, who is about to judge us, knows all accurately, what gain will result to us from the ignorance of men? What then is this, which is yet unspoken? From that day on which you didst impart to me the suspicion of the bishopric, my whole system has often been in danger of being completely unhinged, such was the fear, such the despondency which seized my soul; for on considering the glory of the Bride of Christ, the holiness, the spiritual beauty and wisdom, and comeliness, and then reckoning up my own faults, I used not to cease bewailing both her and myself, and amidst continual distress and perplexity, I kept saying—who then made such a suggestion as this? why has the Church of God made so great a mistake? why has she so provoked her Master, as to be delivered over to me, the unworthiest of all men, and to undergo such great disgrace? Considering these things often by myself and being unable to bear the thought of so monstrous a thing, I used to be like thunderstruck people, speechless, and unable either to see or hear. And when this condition of great helplessness left me, for there were times when it passed off, tears and despondency succeeded to it, and after the flood of tears, then fear again, entered in their stead, disturbing, confusing and agitating my mind. In such a tempest I used to pass the time that is gone; but you was ignorant of it, and thought that I was spending my time in a perfect tranquility, but I will now try and unveil to you the storm of my soul, for it may be you will henceforth pardon me, abandoning your accusations. How then shall I unveil this to you? For if you would see this clearly, it is not otherwise possible than by laying bare my own heart; but as this is impossible, I will try and show you as well as I can, by a certain faint illustration, the gloom of my despondency, and from this image please to infer my condition.

Let us suppose that the daughter of the King of all the earth under the sun is the betrothed of a certain man, and that this damsel has matchless beauty, transcending that of human nature, and that in this respect she outstrips by a long distance the whole race of women; also that she has virtues of the soul, so great as to distance by a long way the whole generation of men that have been, or that shall be; and that the grace of her manners transcends all standards of art, and that the loveliness of her person is eclipsed by the beauty of her countenance; and that her betrothed, not only for the sake of these things, is enamored of the maiden, but apart from these things has an affection for her, and by his ardor throws into the shade the most passionate of lovers that ever were. Then let us suppose, whilst he is burning with love, he hears from some quarter that some mean, abject man, low born, and crippled in body, in fact a thoroughly bad fellow, was about to wed this wondrous, well-be loved maiden. Have we then presented to you some small portion of our grief? and is it enough to stay my illustration at this point? So far as my despondency is concerned, I think it is enough; for this was the only purpose for which I introduced the comparison, but that I may show you the measure of my fear, and my terror, let me proceed to another description.

Let there be an armament composed of infantry, cavalry, and marines, and let a number of triremes cover the sea, and phalanxes of foot and horse cover most of the plains, and the ridges of the mountains, and let the metal of their armor reflect the sunshine, and the glitter of the helmets and shields be reflected by the beams which are emitted from them; let the clashing of spears and the neighing of horses be borne up to the very heavens, and let neither sea nor land appear, but only brass and iron in every direction. Let the enemy be drawn up in battle array opposite to these, fierce and savage men, and let the time of the engagement be now at hand. Then let someone suddenly seize some young lad, one of those brought up in the country, knowing nothing but the use of the shepherd's pipe and crook; let him be clad in brazen armor, and let him be led round the whole camp and be shown the squadrons and their officers, the archers, slingers, captains, generals, the foot and horse, the spearmen, the triremes and their commanders, the dense mass of soldiers in the ships, and the multitude of engines of war lying ready on board. Let him be shown, moreover, the whole array of the enemy, their repulsive aspect, and the varied stores and unusual quantity of their arms, the ravines also and precipices of the mountains, deep and difficult. Let him be shown further on the enemies' side, horses flying by some enchantment and infantry borne through the air, and sorcery of every power and form; and let him consider the calamities of war, the cloud of spears, the hailstorm of arrows, that great mist and obscurity that gloomiest night which the multitude of weapons occasions, eclipsing the sunbeams with their cloud, the dust no less than the darkness baffling the eyesight. The torrents of blood, the groanings of the falling, the shouts of the surviving, the heaps of slain, wheels bathed in blood, horses with their riders thrown headlong down, owing to the number of corpses, the ground a scene of general confusion, blood, and bows, and arrows, hoofs of horses and heads of men lying together, a human arm and a chariot wheel and a helmet, a breast pierced through, brains sticking to swords, the point of a dart broken off with an eye transfixed upon it.

Then let him reckon up the sufferings of the naval force, the triremes burning in the midst of the waves, and sinking with their armed crews, the roaring of the sea, the tumult of the sailors, the shout of the soldiers, the foam of the waves mixed with blood, and dashing over into all the ships; the corpses on the decks, some sinking, some floating, some cast upon the beach, overwhelmed by the waves, and obstructing the passage of the ships. And when he has been carefully instructed in all the tragedy of warfare, let the horrors of captivity and of slavery be added to it, worse than any kind of death; and having told him all this, bid him mount his horse straightway, and take command of all that armament.

Dost you really think that this lad would be equal to more than the mere description, and would not, at the very first glance, lose heart?

13. Do not think that I have exaggerated the matter by my account, nor suppose that because we are shut up in this body, as in some prison house, and are unable to see anything of the invisible world, that what has been said is overstated. For you would see a far greater and more formidable conflict than this, could you ever behold, with these eyes of thine, the devil's most gloomy battle array, and his frantic onset. For there is no brass or iron there. No horses, or chariots or wheels, no fire and darts. These are visible things. But there are other much more fearful engines than these. One does not need against these enemies breastplate or shield, sword and spear, yet the sight only of this accursed array is enough to paralyze the soul, unless it happens to be very noble, and to enjoy in a high degree as a protection to its own courage the providential care of God. And if it were possible by putting off this body, or still keeping it, to see clearly and

fearlessly with the naked eye the whole of his battle array, and his warfare against us, you would see no torrents of blood, nor dead bodies, but so many fallen souls, and such disastrous wounds that the whole of that description of warfare which I just now detailed to you you would think to be mere child's sport and pastime rather than war: so many are there smitten every day, and the wounds in the two cases do not bring about the same death, but as great as is the difference between the soul from the body, so great is the difference between that death and this. For when the soul receives a wound, and falls, it does not lie as a lifeless body, but it is thenceforth tormented, being gnawed by an evil conscience; and after its removal hence, at the time of judgment, it is delivered over to eternal punishment; and if anyone be without grief in regard to the wounds given by the devil, his danger becomes the greater for his insensibility. For whoever is not pained by the first wound, will readily receive a second, and after that a third. For the unclean spirit will not cease assaulting to the last breath, whenever he finds a soul supine and indifferent to his first wounds; and if you would inquire into the method of attack, you would find this much more severe and varied. For no one ever knew so many forms of craft and deceit as that unclean spirit. By this indeed, he has acquired the greater part of his power, nor can anyone have so implacable a hatred against his worst enemies as the evil one against the human race. And if anyone inquire into the vehemence with which he fights, here again it would be ludicrous to bring men into comparison with him. But if any one choose out the fiercest and most savage of beasts, and is minded to set their fury against his, he will find that they were meek and quiet in comparison, such rage does he breathe forth when he attacks our souls; and the period of the warfare indeed in the former case is brief, and in this brief space there are respites; for the approach of the night and the fatigue of slaughter, meal-times also, and many other things, afford a respite to the soldier, so that he can doff his armor and breathe a little, and refresh himself with food and drink, and in many other ways recover his former strength. But in the case of the evil one it is not possible ever to lay aside one's armor, it is not possible even to take sleep, for one who would remain always unscathed. For one of two things must be: either to fall and perish unarmed, or to stand equipped and ever watchful. For he ever stands with his own battle array, watching for our indolence, and laboring more zealously for our destruction, than we for our salvation.

And that he is not seen by us, and suddenly assails us, which things are a source of countless evils to those who are not always on the watch, proves this kind of war to be harder than the other. Could you wish us, then, in such a case to command the soldiers of Christ? yea, this were to command them for the devil's service, for whenever he who ought to marshal and order others is the most inexperienced and feeble of all men, by betraying through this inexperience those who have been entrusted to his charge, he commands them in the devil's interests rather than in Christ's.

But why dost you sigh? why weep? For my ease does not now call for wailing, but for joy and gladness.

Basil: But not my case, yea this calls for countless lamentations. For I am hardly able yet to understand to what degree of evil you hast brought me. For I came to you wanting to learn what excuse I should make on thy behalf to those who find fault with you; but you send me back after putting another case in the place of that I had. For I am no longer concerned about the excuses I shall give them on thy behalf, but what excuse I shall make to God for myself and my own faults. But I beseech you, and implore you, if my welfare is at all regarded by you, if there be any consolation in Christ, if any comfort of love, if any bowels, and mercies, for you knows that thyself above all hast brought me into this danger, stretch forth thine hand, both saying and doing what is able to restore me, do not have the heart to leave me for the briefest moment, but now rather than before let me pass my life with you.

Chrysostom: But I smiled, and said, how shall I be able to help, how to profit you under so great a burden of office? But since this is pleasant to you, take courage, dear soul, for at any time at which it is possible for you to have leisure amid thine own cares, I will come and will comfort you, and nothing shall be wanting of what is in my power.

On this, he weeping yet more, rose up. But I, having embraced him and kissed his head, led him forth, exhorting him to bear his lot bravely. For I believe, said I, that through Christ who has called you, and set you over his own sheep, you wilt obtain such assurance from this ministry as to receive me also, if I am in danger at the last day, into thine everlasting tabernacle.

www.ingramcontent.com/pod-product-compliance
Lightning Source LLC
Chambersburg PA
CBHW071245070526
44583CB00017B/2339